Catholic Men Will Change America:
Advent Reflections from the Frontline

HOLYWATERBOOKS

please check out our
other titles online at
www.holywaterbooks.com

Author's Bio

Joseph Reciniello is one half of a radio show called the Frontline with Joe & Joe, which airs of Veritas Catholic Network, an EWTN affiliate. He has a BS from the University of Scranton, an MS from New Jersey City University & an MBA from St Peter's University. He and his wife Sabryna reside in New Jersey with their five children: Teresa; Francesco; Matteo, Gerard & Maria

Dedicated to my wife Sabryna -
Without her this book would not
have been written - Thank you for
marrying me - I love you

Endorsements

God desires to speak to us through the Sacred Scriptures. This can surprise people. At times, it become more understandable when they have an example and a guide. Joe Reciniello provides that example and gives that guide in his new book, Catholic Men and Their Role in Renewing the Church. I strongly recommend this book to all those who want to encounter God and hear him speak to them through the Sacred Scriptures.

- **Fr. Jeffrey Kirby**, STD Host, Daily Discipleship
with Father Kirby

"The language of God is silence," writes Joe Reciniello. "And our world today is far too noisy." So clear some quiet space for Joe's reflections on daily Mass readings. Enlivened with personal anecdotes, these entries feel like talking to a good and faithful Catholic friend. They should become an essential supplement to your prayer routine; if you don't have one, they might encourage you to begin. And they'll definitely inspire you to seek out a little holy silence every day to digest their wisdom in full.

- **Dan LeRoy** is an author, journalist and teacher
who has been the director of the Writing and
Publishing Department at Lincoln Park Performing
Arts Charter School in Midland, Pennsylvania

This book shows you that God did not design the Bible to be a dark puzzle for bright scholars but to be a bright lamp for travelers through a dark world. This book reminds that when you read the Bible the main things are the plain things, and the plain things are the main things. This book is not meant to make you a Bible scholar, it will make you become a Bible lover. Reading the daily Mass readings should be practiced by new Catholics, lifelong Catholics, Non-Catholics, Revert Catholics and all Catholic Christians. Dr Scott Hahn says we need "to read the bible with the heart of the Church." This book was written by a man who reads the bible with the heart of the Church. This book will show you the impor-tance and benefits of reading the Mass readings everyday.

- **Jesse Romero**, Retired veteran of the Los Angeles County Sheriff's Department Radio Host Author and Catholic Speaker

Joe Reciniello's new book, Reflections from the Frontlines: Catholic Men and Their Role in Renewing the Church, provides daily devotions based on Mass readings, and serves as a guiding light for Catholic men seeking to deepen their faith and actively participate in the Church's renewal. This wonderful collection is a testament to Joe's dedication to inspiring others through thoughtful reflection and spiritual insight. A must-read for those yearning to strengthen their spiritual journey and embrace their role in the Church's mission.

- **Anthony DeStefano**, Bestselling Catholic Author

Joe Reciniello knows that Jesus is the way, the truth and the life. He knows the way and shows it to us. He tells the truth and he tells it like it is. No nonsense. Common sense. Uncommon wisdom. He is a man alive, fully alive, in the life of Christ.

- **Joseph Pearce**, Author of numerous literary studies

I'm a frequent guest on Joe's radio show, and I know this much: An hour now and then is not enough for conversation with the guy. It seems like we're just getting started, and then we're out of time! That's why I'm so happy about this book. It's an easy way to keep the conversation going and talk with Joe while talking with God - all about the most important things in life.

- **Mike Aquilina**, Author, EWTN host, co-founder of the St. Paul Center for Biblical Theology

Joe Reciniello loves Christ and loves his faith, and he shares that love in these meditations inspired by the Scripture readings for daily Mass. His audience is Catholic men (though everyone can benefit), and he offers pragmatic plain advice, straight from the shoulder, prompted by the equally frank words of Jesus: Let's quit slacking off, he says, and fix our spirits on following where the Lord leads--even if that means carrying a cross we think too big to bear. Listeners to the Joe & Joe broadcast on Catholic Veritas will want this book. His voice here rings clear and true: it's just as passionate, caring, and hammer-stroke strong as when you tune in to his radio show. Joe's words will send you back to the Bible and the Mass with fresh insights and fresh devotion in your heart.

- **David Pinault,** Author of *Providence Blue: A Fantasy Quest* and *The Crucifix on Mecca's Front Porch: A Christian's Companion for the Study of Islam*

Joe Reciniello's reflections share the common sense of a man who lives a deeply spiritual life in the midst of "everyman" challenges and the upward yearning of a soul in love with and sold out to God. His reflections give you traction and give you no excuse. As we say in the surf in Hawaii "don't be a poser." He dares us to get real with God.

- **Bear Woznick,** EWTN TV & Radio Host, World Champ Surfer

TABLE OF CONTENTS

Foreword

In a time of uncertainty and turmoil in the world and in the Church, we can thank God that he continues to provide marvelous beacons of wisdom and grace to invigorate our faith and light a fire within us for a strong Catholic commitment. We are seeing some great examples today of "roll-up-your-sleeves" Catholic wise men. I can think of no better figure than Joe Reciniello, who in part learned his trade of spiritual wisdom by years of close contact with the Missionaries of Charity, the Sisters of St. Teresa of Kolkota, and their work with the hard-core, inner city poor. Joe is one half of the very successful radio program, Front Line with Joe and Joe, where, along with Joe Pacillo, these partners in Catholic brotherhood combine wit, wisdom, and sound advice to a large audience of radio listeners in the Metropolitan New York area. It is a very appealing show.

These pages, not surprisingly, are full of the same spiritual power that his radio show displays. The book is a small goldmine of insightful remarks, anecdotes, and commentary on issues that matter most once we face God more directly. As a priest, I must say how refreshing it is to read a layman like Joe comment on the Scripture and the Gospels when in contrast we may be hearing too many sermons from the pulpit a bit unconcerned with Jesus Christ and the ultimate importance of salvation and God. This lack of focus is not a problem on these pages. Joe hits his target in each of these meditations and reflections with verve and gusto. We are left remembering his words and images because he speaks so directly. His stories from his personal life, and his knowledge of saints and recent history, all fuel an animated, lively presentation. The conversational style leaves one calling Joe a good friend by the end of this book.

Most importantly, Joe leads us to love our Catholic faith. He shows clearly what Catholic commitment can do to foster stability and happiness in our vocational pursuits and energize our lives. Joe is a married man dedicated to his wife and children and this dimension of sacrificial life as a husband and father is a core truth of this man. I have known him from his days as a volunteer with the Missionaries of Charity before his marriage. Now he is an even greater man. He is a wonderful testimony to the truth that faithfulness in lifelong marriage and fatherhood is a sure path to happiness and closeness to God. Many young men, and young women as well, can learn much in this regard by reading these pages. A final word on this fine book: on the one hand, we can take delight in these reflections of this Franciscan of the Third Millenium, smiling often in enjoyment at what we read. Or we can go further and seek a path to wisdom ourselves in a deeper life of prayer and Catholic faithfulness, which is what Joe has done himself in his life. May God bless Joe Reciniello and his family and all who read this wonderful book!

Father Donald Haggerty,
St. Patrick's Cathedral, NYC

1ˢᵗ
Day of Advent

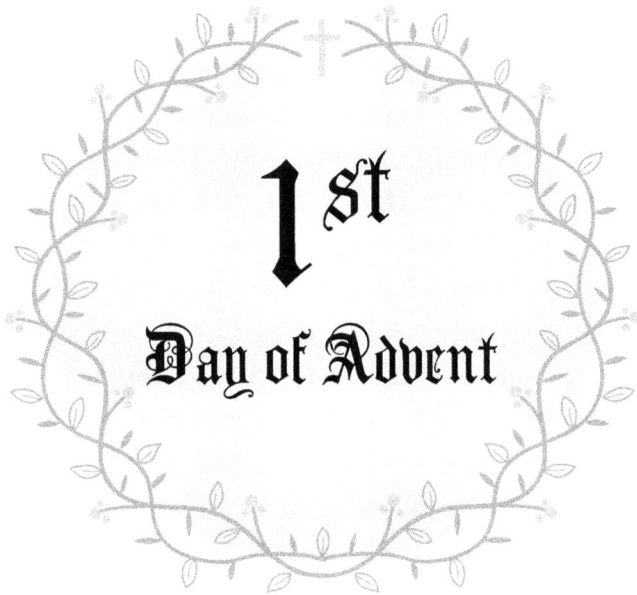

THE KING OF KINGS WAS BORN IN
A BARN....ARE WE WILLING TO FIND
HIM THERE?......IN THE WORLD OF
THE FORGOTTEN......BORN IN A BARN,
CHRIST CAME INTO THE WORLD

Today Advent begins in the Universal Church . A time to prepare for the birth of Jesus Christ Advent is like a "mini" Lent A time to increase our prayers and fasting to focus our mind and heart towards Christ's birth . During this time I often spend some time sitting before a Nativity scene after daily Mass . The statue of the Child Jesus is not in the manger yet but Joseph and Mary are there Siting in a barn full of animals ..During the time I spend kneeing before the Nativity I think just how hard is was for Joseph and Mary They were fully human They had so much faith and trust but that did not take away what they had to endure and what they were up against .Then here comes baby Jesus, the King of Kings Born poor and born for the entire world The Nativity scene, set up in Catholic Churches around the world during Advent is in a sense a mirror image of what our hearts should look like before the birth of the Christ-Child on Christmas Day - Humble When we acknowledge out own "poverty" before God - God "raises us up" and fills us with Himself.

"Your ways, O LORD, make known to me; teach me your paths, Guide me in your truth and teach me, for you are God my savior, and for you I wait all the day"

Its hard for me sometimes to focus on the true spirit of Christmas in the New York Metropolitan Area…So much "flash" and "bling"….. Before I was married I would spend the three weeks before Christmas in India serving the poor with Mother Teresa's sisters….

There was no "flash" and "bling" there....When I would fly out of JFK airport in New York and land in Kolkata it was like flying back into time....Life was "stripped down".....I lived, ate and saw a side of life that is so different from what I was used to in New York.... Coming from the "flash" and "bling" of a New York Christmas and landing into a third world city always made me reflect...It helped me to "enter into" Advent...To prepare my heart for the birth of the Savior of the World............In every city there is what is commonly referred to as an "under-belly", where a segment of society lives what is invisible to the rest of "polite society".....Even where we live in New York / New Jersey....You do not have to go too far to find this "under-belly".......This was the segment of the world Jesus entered......Born in a barn - The first people to find him were shepherds in fields, the lowest rung of society.....Many times its in this "under-belly" of cities around the world where the Catholic faith is strongest......On Wednesday's in Lower Manhattan the Missionaries of Charity would give out food to shut-ins living in boarding houses above storefronts in Chinatown...I have gone with them there a number of times....My eyes could not believe how people in my city, one of the richest cities in the world lived - Living in closets with next to nothing - I remember this one man who would only open his door a crack to receive the food the Sisters gave to him...He was clearly mentally handicapped and all alone in this world...This is the world Mary and Joseph entered when they gave birth to the King of Kings....The world of the forgotten......Born in a barn, Christ came into the world for us......I have learned that we do not have to fly halfway around the world to "find the Christ child" as I would do before I was married...Jesus can be found broken and alone right on the street you live on!.... In order to find him we must "enter into" Christ's poverty making our hearts humble, recognizing our own poverty, which we "mask" with "flash" and "bling".....It's there we will encounter something we never knew existed

"Good and upright is the LORD; thus he shows sinners the way. He guides the humble to justice, and teaches the humble his way"

So the question today is...How will you make this Advent special?...How will you prepare your heart for the birth of the King of Kings?....."Then the LORD said: Go out and stand on the mountain before the LORD; the LORD will pass by. There was a strong and violent wind rending the mountains and crushing rocks before the LORD—but the LORD was not in the wind; after the wind, an earthquake—but the LORD was not in the earthquake. After the earthquake, fire—but the LORD was not in the fire; after the fire, a light silent sound".......Christ is found in the "under-belly" of our heart....Under our "mask".....In the "flash" and "bling" of what we Americans know to be Christmas we will not find him.... The King of Kings was born in a barn....Are we willing to find him there?......In the world of the forgotten......Born in a barn, Christ came into the worldrist came into the world.

PERSONAL NOTES:

2nd

Day of Advent

"I REJOICED BECAUSE THEY SAID
TO ME, "WE WILL GO UP TO THE
HOUSE OF THE LORD."

Today at Holy Mass we hear in the first reading from the Prophet Isaiah .."In days to come, The mountain of the LORD's house shall be established as the highest mountain and raised above the hills. All nations shall stream toward it" .Isaiah is giving his people and us as well something to hope for .There is something better on the horizon ..And only Jesus can deliver it .All of us are flawed and everything we touch as human beings are consequently flawed as well People and governments since the beginning of time try to create "heaven on earth" in so many different ways All of those efforts ultimately fail .Christ is the "missing piece" that our humanity requires All people whether they realize it or not are incomplete Until we realize this and accept the one who only can complete us We will be like a dog chasing its tail Whether on Central Park South in Manhattan, in a hut in Tanzania or in housing projects on the Southside of Chicago .. The human race was made by God and when God is rejected, something breaks within us .This is reality .And this reality is visible to all ..The only thing that stands in our way of "filling in the missing piece" is our pride

"Many will come from the east and the west, and will recline with Abraham, Isaac, and Jacob at the banquet in the Kingdom of heaven"

All people need hope...Something to look forward too... Something to strive for...Once a person loses that hope - They are finished…..As we get older we realize all the "things" of this earth do not fully satisfy…..Whether it was career advancement, academic achievement or even in the people we love…..Nothing and no one is perfect…That reality should tell us something…We were created for "something" else……….Life has a way of humbling people…And its when we embrace humility….Realize and accept our limitations…And acknowledge our weakness…Its than that a "door" opens and God awaits on the other side of that door….. Billy McGill was born poor in Liverpool England…He left home at 16 to be a Longshoreman never to return to his native country again…..I got to know Billy where I would attend daily Mass a number of years ago in Lyndhurst New Jersey…Billy was a "rough guy"…He lost his family…He lost his house…And when I met him after digging himself out of the hole he created…Starting all over…He found his Catholic faith and was a daily communicant at the Church I attended…..Look at what it took for Billy to get where God could work with him?……In many ways and for many people, this is what it takes…..Rock Bottom!……God allows us to pursue "everything" we "think" we want and need….And when we get it…We find that it does not fully satisfy…I would go to Giant Football games with Billy before he died…..As an older guy, he was very generous and if you met him you would never know the life he once led……Billy eventually got cancer and my wife and I would visit him in the hospital shortly before he passed away…He told me as he was lying in his bed he could hear the man in the bed next to him crying out as he was about to die…Billy told me with tears in his eyes he prayed the Divine Mercy Chaplet for the man silently and was assured that Christ took mercy on his soul…Billy lived a rough life and was not dealt the best hand…He made big mistakes and when he "hit rock bottom" he found God and in finding God he found peace…..I think of Billy often and I have peace when I think about him knowing Jesus took care of him....Billy was a Longshoreman and construction worker...And Jesus was a Carpenter....Jesus always takes care of his own!

"Come and save us, LORD our God; Let your face shine upon us, that we may be saved"

The Prophet Isaiah reminds us today at Mass...."They shall beat their swords into plowshares and their spears into pruning hooks; One nation shall not raise the sword against another, nor shall they train for war again".....The hope of the human race is not found in "things"...Its only found in God.....Mankind still has not "bought in"....Like a dog chasing its tail....Chasing after one thing after the next....When I first got married Billy would stop over my house and give me advice like he was my father.....One day I offered him a Guinness beer.....Billy used to drink a lot but not any more... He kindly turned the beer down, looked at me as he smiled and said..."In every bottle of Guinness beer Joe there is a baby"...Once again Billy was right....My wife and I had five children in ten years of marriage.......The Longshoreman from Liverpool England "figured it out"....With a smile on his face and his Divine Mercy Chaplet in his hand...He figured it out!

"I rejoiced because they said to me, "We will go up to the house of the LORD."

PERSONAL NOTES:

3rd

Day of Advent

GOD CAN DO SO MUCH MORE WITH
YOUR LIFE THEN YOU CAN DO WITH
IT....."OUR LORD SHALL COME WITH
POWER; HE WILL ENLIGHTEN THE
EYES OF HIS SERVANTS"

Today the Universal Church honors St Francis Xavier, a founding member of the Jesuit Order and missionary to Asia .Francis Xavier met Ignatius Loyola at the University of Paris ..Francis Xavier came from a noble Spanish family as did Ignatius Loyola, he was a great athlete and a scholar ..He had a wonderful life of wealth, power and prestige in front of him ..Instead he chose a different path .."He emptied himself, taking the form of a slave .He humbled himself becoming obedient to death .Because of this, God greatly exalted him" .Francis Xavier encounter the living God and this encountered changed the course of his life .Any person who encounters Truth incarnate is never the same ..And because of this encounter the world was not the same St Francis Xavier brought the Catholic faith to India, Sri Lanka, Malaysia & Japan .His impact in the Christian world is second only to St Paul as far as the miles he traveled and the souls he converted to Christ .All because of his encounter with the Carpenter from Nazareth .What makes the son of a noble family give-up everything the world has to offer? The answer was clear to Francis Xavier - Such a person does not give up such a life for a myth or lie

"A shoot shall sprout from the stump of Jesse, and from his roots a bud shall blossom"

As Catholics it's so important to familiarize ourselves with the lives of the saints....The saints were real people who did incredible things….What was their secret?…They had an authentic encounter with Christ…Far too many people view Jesus as just a word…He was just some "guy" who lived 2000 years ago to many…But if you step back and think about how millions upon millions of people have changed their lives because of Jesus Christ - Its simply hard to grasp….Jesus said he was the Truth…And each of us deeply desires to live a life of Truth - But we are afraid…...When someone speaks the Truth, something resonates deep within the human heart

"He shall rescue the poor when he cries out, and the afflicted when he has no one to help him. He shall have pity for the lowly and the poor; the lives of the poor he shall save."

Before we can be filled with God, we must empty ourself…This is what the saints did and do….As a 54 year old man I have seen many people come and go in my life…I always marvel at how I knew a person in one chapter of my life and now that same person chang-es….Marriage is one of those "encounters" with Truth…Marriage changes a man…He becomes selfless…He lives for his wife and children…Marriage is a Sacrament and God helps a man to make this change…I have seen this many times in my life…A person I knew "changed" once he got married…..Similarly, if we take our Catholic faith seriously and allow the grace of the Sacraments, daily prayer and fasting to take hold of our life, we too will change….St Paul puts it this way…."Yet I live, no longer I, but Christ lives in me; insofar as I now live in the flesh, I live by faith in the Son of God who has loved me and given himself up for me"…..This kind of "change" is very real and is available to us all…..We see this example in the lives of the saints but also in many Catholic couples who live their marriage Sacramentally…This is the road to heaven…"To die to ourself"…Far too many people have a misconception of what it means to "go to heaven"…..What do you mean

Joe?.......The road to heaven is a constant call to die to ourself.....
But I believe in Jesus Joe, isn't that enough?.....Of course we must
believe in Jesus, but if we do not try to imitate the life of Christ and
live what he taught - Then "Jesus" is simple just "a guy" or a word
that gets "thrown around" a lot......The saints show us this lived
example in real time...And as a result, God uses them...God can
use us too if we let him.

On that day, The root of Jesse, set up as a signal for the nations, The
Gentiles shall seek out, for his dwelling shall be glorious.

St Francis Xavier shook the foundations of the world because he
fully embraced the will of God and emptied himself, allowing the
Holy Spirit to empower him....If he did not say "Yes" to the Lord,
he would have been just another "rich kid" who went to a good col-
lege and made money when he got out - No different then today...
Instead, Francis Xavier chose a different path and countless lives
were changed because of his choice - His YES....This "path" is
available to each of us....When you have been blessed with an education and come from a good family, like St Francis Xavier, its very
easy to choose the path laid out for you - The path we all have been
indoctrinated to take by our society....However, if we really want
to make a difference...And deep down everyone wants to make
an impact...Then we must "Let-go" and "Let God"...This kind of
choice begins with an authentic encounter with the living God...
Because God is real...People do not give up wonderful lives for a
myth or a lie.....So why settle for second best?.....God can do so
much more with your life then you can do with it.....'"Our Lord
shall come with power; he will enlighten the eyes of his servants"

PERSONAL NOTES:

4th
Day of Advent

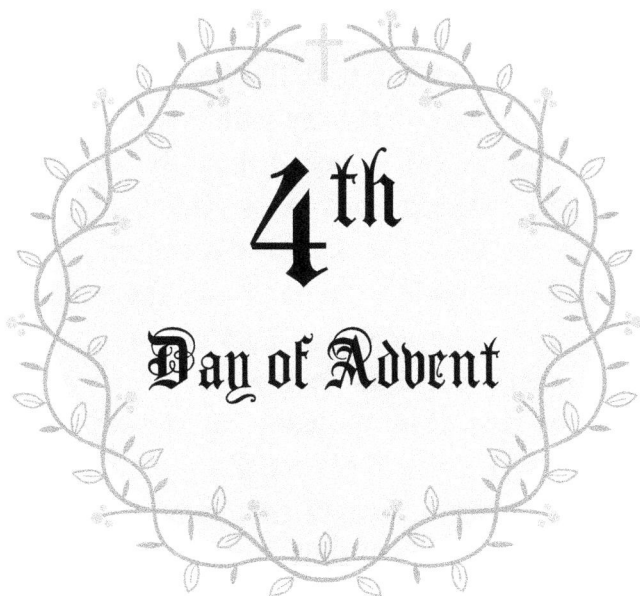

PAY ATTENTION, THIS IS ON THE
FINAL EXAM....."COME, YOU WHO
ARE BLESSED BY MY FATHER.
INHERIT THE KINGDOM PREPARED
FOR YOU FROM THE FOUNDATION OF
THE WORLD. FOR I WAS HUNGRY AND
YOU GAVE ME FOOD"

Today at Holy Mass we hear in the Gospel of St Matthew how Jesus felt compassion for his people, they were hungry so he fed them Such a basic idea His response is so natural They were hungry so he fed them ."Jesus summoned his disciples and said, My heart is moved with pity for the crowd, for they have been with me now for three days and have nothing to eat. I do not want to send them away hungry, for fear they may collapse on the way" ..Everything Jesus does in the Gospel is done for a reason - He is giving us an example and we are meant to do the same - Just as he did ..No one ever became poor by sharing ..And if we each did our part, there would be no one who goes without in this world Have you ever been "in want" of something? Have you ever been hungry? Many times its the poor, who understand what it means to share because they know what it means to be hungry - Because they lived it ..When we were students in high school our teachers would say "Pay attention, this will be on the final exam" ..Well, Jesus was the greatest teacher who ever lived ..And this is what he is telling us today - It should be crystal clear - So pay attention   "When the Son of Man comes in his glory, and all the angels with him, he will sit upon his glorious throne, and all the nations will be assembled before him. And he will separate them one from another, as a shepherd separates the sheep from the goats. He will place the sheep on his right and the goats on his left. Then the king will say to those on his right, 'Come, you who are blessed by my Father. Inherit the kingdom prepared for you from the foundation of the world. For I was hungry and you gave me food, I was thirsty and you gave me drink, a stranger and you welcomed me, naked and you clothed me, ill and you cared for me, in prison and you visited me.' Then the righteous will answer him and say, 'Lord, when did we see you hungry and feed you, or thirsty and give you drink? When did we see you a stranger and welcome you, or naked and clothe you? When did we see you ill or in prison, and visit you?' And the king will say to them in reply, 'Amen, I say to you, whatever you did for one of these least brothers of mine, you did for me.' Then he will say to those on his left, 'Depart from me, you accursed, into the eternal fire prepared for the devil and his angels. For I was hungry and you gave me no food, I was thirsty and you gave me no drink, a stranger and you gave me no welcome, naked and you gave me no clothing, ill and in prison, and you did not care for me.' Then they will answer and say, 'Lord, when did we see you hungry or thirsty or a stranger or naked or ill or in prison, and not minister to your needs?' He will answer them, 'Amen, I say to you, what you did not do for one of these least ones, you did not do for me.' And these will go off to eternal punishment, but the righteous to eternal life."

"The crowds were amazed when they saw the mute speaking, the deformed made whole, the lame walking, and the blind able to see, and they glorified the God of Israel."

Jesus was a Jew and if you have some knowledge about what it means to be a practicing Jew you will know that they have a lot of laws…Jesus, a good Jew distilled the law into two bullets…….."Love

God above all things and love your neighbor as your self"…Why bring this up?…Because before we can love our neighbor correctly, we must first love God…Because if we do, we will see God in our neighbor and if we see God in our neighbor, we will treat are neighbor well….As a father of five, I cannot watch children suffer, whether its on television or with my own eyes…Because when I see a child suffer, I immediately think of my own children….Having my own children changed my prospective…We too need to change our prospective…We need to see God in others…Then and only when will we reach out a hand to help them when they are in need…..Years ago when I was the driver for the Missionaries of Charity in New York there was this family living on the first floor in the Elliott-Chelsea Housing Projects in Lower Manhattan….A single mother lived there with her 8 children…One of the Missionaries of Charity would always ask me to drive over to their apartment to bring them trays of food…When I would go there the window was always open in the family's apartment and I would call up from the sidewalk to Louis, who was one of the eight kids to come down to the street and bring the food up to his family……..Louis was such a nice young boy and he would always come down……I always remember Louis and years later after I was married I was visiting the sisters and asked one of the nuns about Louis…She told me he was in jail, Rikers Island to be exact…This news broke my heart…I had my own children at this point and remembered Louis as such an innocent little boy when I would call up to him…Now he was in jail….Thinking about it makes me want to cry to this day…..Again most especially now because I am a Father of five and have three boys of my own……..Why mention this story?.....God looks at all of us as his children…And God weeps when we hurt or are in need, like any parent would……God appreciates when we assist his children in need, as we would if someone helped one of our own children.....Before I had my own kids, I looked at young Louis differently...He was just some "poor kid"...Someone else's kid... Now that I have my own kids, I see all children differently...My prospective has changed....We too must "change" our prospective in how we "see" others.....In order to "see", we must take to heart the first two commandments Jesus gave to us....."Love God above all things and love your neighbor as your self"....We will never "see" our neighbor or feel we need to reach out a hand to help him until we learn to see God in our neighbor....How can we learn to "see" in this manner?...If we can see Jesus, who is fully present in the Blessed Sacrament...Body, Blood, Soul and Divinity.....Then we will see Jesus in our neighbor....Our prospective will change and when our prospective changes, the world around us will change as well.

"Then he took the seven loaves and the fish, gave thanks, broke the loaves, and gave them to the disciples, who in turn gave them to the crowds. They all ate and were satisfied"

St Matthew today in the Gospel tells us about Jesus feeding others.....Why did he do it?...Because he cared for his people...Do we care about others?...Do we see Jesus in others?.......Some people think that this mindset is optional....Once again, St Matthew reminds us that helping others is not optional...In fact, in our "exit interview" before God when we die, how we treated our neighbor will be front and center during the conversation.....'Amen, I say to you, whatever you did for one of these least brothers of mine, you did for me."....Back to what our high school teachers would tell us, "Pay attention, this is on the final exam".....'"Come, you who are blessed by my Father. Inherit the kingdom prepared for you from the foundation of the world. For I was hungry and you gave me food"

PERSONAL NOTES:

5th
Day of Advent

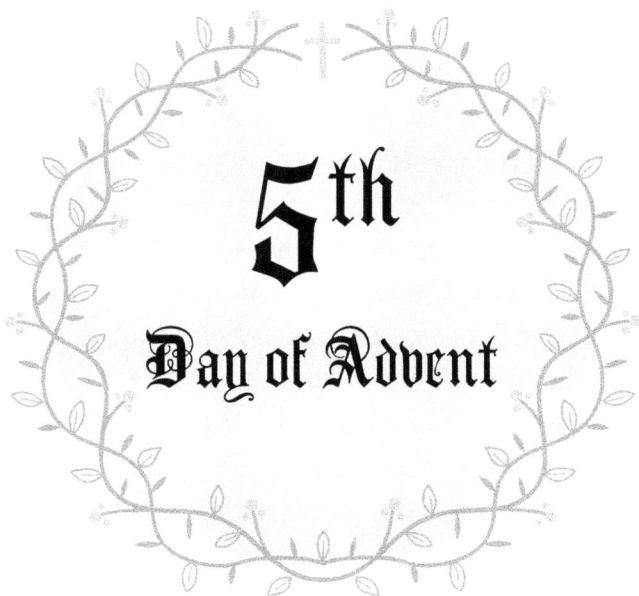

"EVERY GOOD TREE BEARS GOOD FRUIT, AND A ROTTEN TREE BEARS BAD FRUIT. A GOOD TREE CANNOT BEAR BAD FRUIT, NOR CAN A ROTTEN TREE BEAR GOOD FRUIT.".....
STILL DON'T BELIEVE ME?

Today at Holy Mass we hear in the in the Gospel of St Matthew the "blue print" of how to build a good and fruitful life ..But before we "build" this life We must be convinced that "God's way" is better then our way .Most people are not convinced .We "think" we figured it out" We "think" we are so "smart" We "think" God's way is outdated ..The problem is we "think" too much .A holy nun once told me "Joe - Stop thinking so much - Just pray and do!" "Everyone who listens to these words of mine and acts on them will be like a wise man who built his house on rock. The rain fell, the floods came, and the winds blew and buffeted the house. But it did not collapse; it had been set solidly on rock. And everyone who listens to these words of mine but does not act on them will be like a fool who built his house on sand. The rain fell, the floods came, and the winds blew and buffeted the house. And it collapsed and was completely ruined."

"Seek the LORD while he may be found; call him while he is near."

The American mindset is fiercely independent...That is a good thing - To a degree.....However, no matter who we are or how gifted we may be...We were created by God and without God as Scripture tells us we can do nothing that will last.....Most people have to figure this out by first trying it their way....And fail.... Making mistakes is a part of every human life...However, as I tell my children...."We all make mistakes, the key is to learn from them" - Those who learn from their mistakes lead successful lives and those who double-down on their mistakes do not"......Take that statement to the bank!.....Years ago I met a friend of mine who is the Godfather of one of my children...Michael came from a family, which had no religion at all. His parents were divorced and Michael lived a crazy life as a young man....His story about how he became Catholic and turned his life around is amazing... Michael as a young man partied a lot and one day after drinking too much, he got into a very bad car accident and was in the hospital for two months...During that time in the hospital, he decided to become Catholic and get Baptized...Kind of crazy how the idea came into his head because he had experienced no religion at all from his family or friends, yet this "idea" came to him and he followed through with it - God works in mysterious ways!....Sadly once Michael became Catholic that was not the end of his crazy life...Michael got married and continued to party and his marriage was not Sacramental...He had one child with his then wife and the child was born handicapped....After seven years his son died..........This put Michael "over the edge"...His marriage fell apart and he knew he was in trouble....So a friend of his told him to speak with a priest, which he did...The priest told Michael to go on a Pilgrimage....Which he did...That is where Michael and I met....From there we became fast friends....Michael began to "dig himself out" of his bad habits...He became a daily communicant (went to Mass every day)...Developed a prayer life.......Gave of his time to the poor......Stopped all the partying........And slowly God began to work in his life...After about seven years of this... Michael met another woman, this time he went about the relationship the right way...His first marriage was not Sacramental so he got an annulment from the Church...He did not "sleep" with his girlfriend before marriage and finally he got married in a small ceremony in the Catholic Church in West New York…Michael now is very happy - A changed man for sure!…He went from a crazy party guy, who almost killed himself in car accident, he endured the death of his son whom he loved with all his heart, a failed marriage… Only to find God, become Catholic, get married within the Church and live a new life built upon the gospel, which we hear from Mass today…..”Everyone who listens to these words of mine and acts on them will be like a wise man who built his house on rock. The rain fell, the floods came, and the winds blew and buffeted the house. But it did not collapse; it had been set solidly on rock”…Michael’s story is not unlike many of our stories…Michael had to “try it his way”…Only to fail….In his misery he found God…….He discovered that God loved him…..He re-built his life upon the “rock” of his Catholic faith…And the rest of history!

“Open to me the gates of justice; I will enter them and give thanks to the LORD”

St Matthew today lays out the “blue print” to a good life…A life built upon the will of God….Our Catholic faith is time tested… Two thousand years of wisdom, of which we can learn from…..God gives us his Church and his Truth, which protects us from our biggest and most fierce enemy - Our very self!……Still don’t believe me?….You don’t have to look too far to see the mistakes of humanity…How people refuse to learn from mistakes…How they double down and triple down on the same behavior “thinking” somehow the outcome will be “different this time”…..I stand before you today and say this…”God’s ways work!…..How do you know I am not lying to you?…St Matthew again gives us the answer….”Beware of false prophets, who come to you in sheep’s clothing, but underneath are ravenous wolves. By their fruits you will know them. Do people pick grapes from thorn-bushes, or figs from thistles? Just so, every good tree bears good fruit, and a rotten tree bears bad fruit. A good tree cannot bear bad fruit, nor can a rotten tree bear good fruit."….. Still don't believe me?

PERSONAL NOTES:

6th
Day of Advent

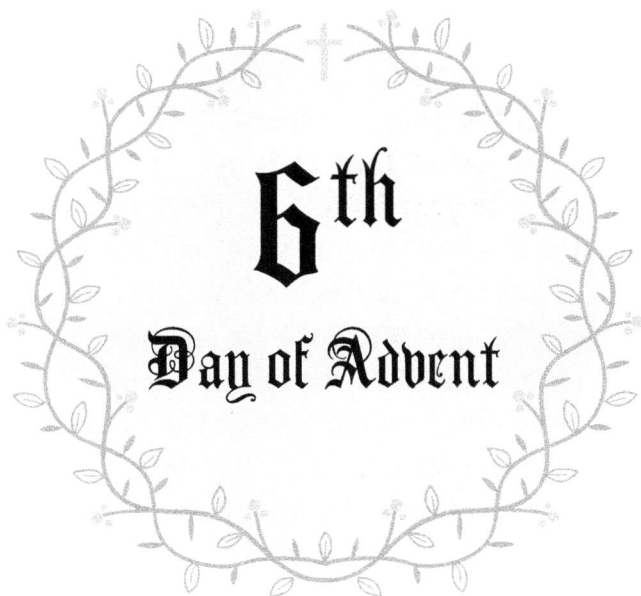

WE NEED TO GIVE HIM PERMISSION
TO MOVE THE "MOUNTAIN" WHICH
EXISTS BETWEEN OUR HEAD AND
OUR HEART....JESUS ASKS US
TODAY....."DO YOU BELIEVE THAT I
CAN DO THIS?"

Today at Holy Mass we hear in the Gospel of St Matthew Jesus addressing people who ask for the impossible Jesus is God, which means he can do anything Do we put God in a box? Do we think of Jesus purely on human terms? When Jesus asks this question today ("Do you believe that I can do this?") the people respond ."Yes, Lord," they said to him. Then he touched their eyes and said, "Let it be done for you according to your faith." .Scripture tells us that if we have "faith the size of a mustard seed" we can tell a mountain to move and it will move ..Many times that "mountain" can be our own heart The greatest distance one can travel is from ones head to their heart But fear not All we need is faith "the size of a mustard seed" ..If we nurture the faith we have, God can move mountains We may even find that the "mountain" he moves is us! Our God is the God of the impossible He rose from the dead and he has "cracked tougher nuts" then you .."O you of little faith"

"On that day the deaf shall hear the words of a book; And out of gloom and darkness, the eyes of the blind shall see"

Americans value achievement - And that is a good thing.....We want our children to get great educations, become professionals and make a good living....Parents condition their children for this outcome.....While achievements such as education and professional success are important....Are we as parents "planting the seeds of faith" within the hearts of our children?....This is BY FAR the most important thing we can give to our kids….A solid Catholic formation will guide all their big decisions in life…Who they marry?…. How they work?…What they do for work?….How they spend their time?…What they spend their time on?…How they spend their money?…I can go on and on…..Passing our Catholic faith on to our children does not happen magically and ultimately a successful life ends with our kids entering the gates of heaven…To the surprise of many…One does not just "float into heaven"….Going to heaven requires a daily decision, which stems from our faith in God…Our faith in God comes from our parents more times then not and if we as parents do not model this faith in the home, we should not expect our children to live as Catholics in the world….. Many years ago on Good Friday my family and I were in our mini-van driving to the 3:00pm prayer service, which takes place every Good Friday…As you know, Good Friday is one of the holiest days of the year…The day Jesus gave his life for the world…If Jesus did not die for us…NO ONE enters heaven…So as a result, Good Friday is a very special day…..Back to the mini-van….On this one Good Friday me and the family were driving to Church for the 3:00pm service and we passed the baseball field in my hometown on the way…It was 2:45pm…Its GOOD FRIDAY…..And a baseball practice was taking place…As we drove by it I thought to myself…How terribly sad…"Our priorities" were on full display and this small example can be seen each and everyday by what we see on television, how our children dress, what they view on their phone……How we spend our time and what we do with our money says everything the world needs to know…It also demonstrates to our children what is important to us, which in turn will form in them what will be important to them when they become adults…… Even if we have faith the size of a mustard seed as Scripture tells us, that faith will not magically grow if we do not tend to it

"They shall keep my name holy; they shall reverence the Holy One of Jacob, and be in awe of the God of Israel"

Jesus today in St Matthew's gospel asks a question.....“Do you believe that I can do this?”......We ask God for “things” all the time.....But in the end we need to realize that God is not a “candy machine” where we put in our “coin” and out pops what we want..... God is our loving father, he made us, knowing that is not where it should end, its where it should begin....Our faith will not grow if we do not nurture it....And our Catholic faith will not be passed down to our children if we do not practice it each day in the home....God can surely “move mountains”.....But before he does, we need to give him permission to move the “mountain” which exists between our head and our heart....Jesus asks us today.....“Do you believe that I can do this?”

PERSONAL NOTES:

7th

Day of Advent

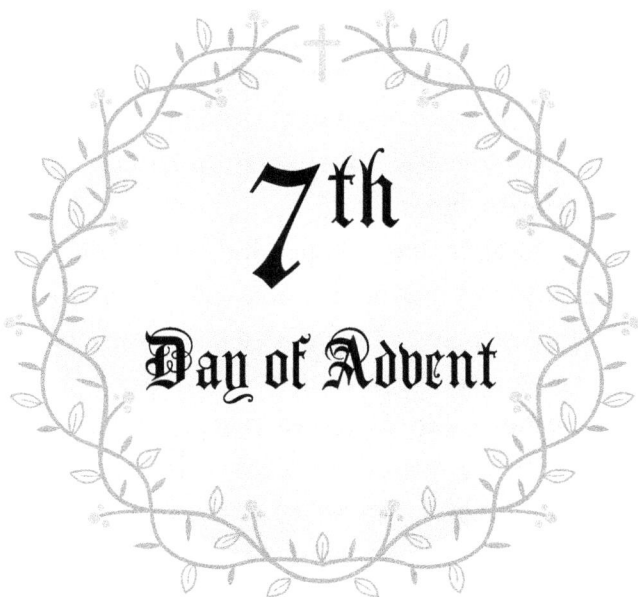

"A MAN WHO WAS GOING ON A JOURNEY CALLED IN HIS SERVANTS AND ENTRUSTED HIS POSSESSIONS TO THEM. TO ONE HE GAVE FIVE TALENTS; TO ANOTHER, TWO; TO A THIRD, ONE—TO EACH ACCORDING TO HIS ABILITY...WHICH MAN ARE YOU AND WHAT WILL YOU DO WITH YOUR GOD GIVEN TALENTS?

Today at Holy Mass we hear in St Matthew's Gospel Jesus instructing his friends .."Without cost you have received; without cost you are to give" .It is very easy to take for granted everything God has given to us Our family .. Our health The country we were born into .So many people in the world do not have what we have and live in and under very difficult conditions So the first question to consider is Do we recognize the gifts, which God has given to us? ..Because if we view them as gifts, we will do what Jesus said today in the gospel ..... ."Without cost you are to give" .And if you do not view what has been given to you as a gift, frankly you will not give ..Some never consider that in a "hot New York minute" everything we have can be taken from us! - You don't think so? ..One visit to the doctor and poof - The party is over! One car accident and poof - The party is over! .Our time here on earth is limited God gave us gifts, not to be hoarded but to be shared Because one day, the "party" will end and God will ask us point blank "What did you do with the gifts I gave you?" . And when that time comes, God will expect a good answer

"The harvest is abundant but the laborers are few; so ask the master of the harvest to send out laborers for his harvest."

In the Parable of the Talents in St Matthew's gospel a story is told about three people....."It will be as when a man who was going on a journey called in his servants and entrusted his possessions to them. To one he gave five talents; to another, two; to a third, one—to

each according to his ability. Then he went away. Immediately"…
This story is something we should all pay attention too…..All people are not equal, what I mean by that is, some people have been given much more than others…Whether they are physically stronger, born into wealthy families, born with brilliant minds, etc.… For example, if a man can throw a baseball 110 miles an hour as a major league pitcher, that is a gift…The average person can not "practice their way" to throwing a baseball 110 miles an hour… With that said, God expects that gifted Major League Baseball player to use that gift to help others who may not be as "gifted"… Sadly that is not the way it works and I am not pointing fingers here at profession well paid athletes.…All of mankind easily loses sight of what has been given to them by God and tends to keep for themself the bounty of their gifts…We see this all around us - I see it in myself…..Do you think God is blind to this?……..A friend of mine who is a priest once told me…If everyone in the world shared, no one would be hungry…As we all know again, that does not happen…I will also ask you again…..Do you think God is blind to this?…Do you think that when mankind stands before God this will not be addressed?…Mother Teresa once said…If you can not feed one hundred people - Feed one...If everyone in the world viewed their gifts in this manner, the world would be a better place for sure…….When I was traveling a lot for work years ago I found myself auditing an office in Beverly Hills…I was in California for two weeks and I stayed over the weekend to enjoy the nice weather…On that particular Sunday, I went to Mass in Beverly Hills… As I walked from my hotel to the Church and passed all the beautiful homes I thought to my self - Who lives here? - Beverly Hills is a far cry from New Jersey where I grew up…..That Sunday Mass in Beverly Hills was well attended and when it came time to line up to receive Holy Communion, the priest did something I never saw

before…I assume he did this every Sunday…Instead of the people in the first aisle of the Church receiving the Blessed Sacrament first, the line began from the back of the Church…..The priest in establishing this tradition at this wealthy parish was trying to teach his people something…"Those who have been given much, much will be expected" - "God came to serve not to be served"…….Write what I just said down!…….When we die and face the Lord, He is going to ask each of us….."When I was hungry - Did you feed me?"…"When I was thirsty - Did you give me a drink?"…."When I was naked - Did you cloth me?"…Now again, I can't do what the people who attended that Mass in Beverly Hills can do…But make no mistake about it - I can do something!…And so can you….. Before that happens, we must see Christ in others…Our hearts of stone must be turned into hearts of flesh…We have to see our time here on earth as something that is temporary….We must view everything we have, each of our talents and material gains as gifts… Once we do that, our hands will open and so will our hearts…Joy will flood into our soul and so will peace….This is how we were intended to live….This is how God made us to be…..No one ever become poor by sharing

"O people of Zion, who dwell in Jerusalem, no more will you weep; He will be gracious to you when you cry out, as soon as he hears he will answer you"

Today Jesus in the Gospel reminds his friends that they have been given so much….And that what was given to them in turn must be shared with others…..I have often thought how blessed we are to be Catholic…To receive the grace of the Sacraments….This is the greatest gift given to mankind - Jesus himself - Body, Blood, Soul and Divinity in the Blessed Sacrament…..We learn from Our Lady when at the Annunciation she said YES to God and Christ entered her womb - And once she received that gift, she immediately "went out" to give it away to her cousin Elizabeth who was in need… It was simple gesture…Elizabeth was pregnant and needed help and Mary her cousin went to help her - So simple…….Mary "saw" Elizabeth's need because her "eyes were open"…….Our eyes too must be opened to the gift, which was given to us…Our very life is a gift!…..And when we recognize our life to be a gift, we too will strive to "give it away"….....This is the path to heaven….."A man who was going on a journey called in his servants and entrusted his possessions to them. To one he gave five talents; to another, two; to a third, one—to each according to his ability…Which man are you and what will you do with your God given talents?

PERSONAL NOTES:

8th

Day of Advent

ARE WE PREPARED?......READY OR
NOT......HERE I COME

Today at Holy Mass we hear in the Gospel of St Luke a prophetic statement ..Jesus, the savior of the world is coming But before he comes ..St Luke gives us a quote from the Old Testament from the Book of Isaiah ."A voice of one crying out in the desert: "Prepare the way of the Lord, make straight his paths. Every valley shall be filled and every mountain and hill shall be made low. The winding roads shall be made straight, and the rough ways made smooth, and all flesh shall see the salvation of God" As we all know, those were the words of John the Baptist but those words echo throughout history to this day Advent is a time to prepare To prepare ourselves for the coming of the Christ Child .. Christmas commemorates each year the brith of Jesus But one day A day we do not know when Jesus will return .Because of that We must prepare

"Although they go forth weeping, carrying the seed to be sown, They shall come back rejoicing, carrying their sheaves"

All human beings die, this is reality…Each of us however were not born to die…We were born to live……Jesus on the other hand was born to die…That was his purpose…He was born to humble parents, to be raised to manhood only to die and his death changed the world forever….When someone dies, the people who love that person always mourn…..And when Jesus died, even his closet friends did not understand…Jesus told them time and time again that he would rise from the dead in three days…But his friends heard the words but did not understand....The only person I think who did understand was his Mother....In Mel Gibson's film the Passion of the Christ as Jesus was being murdered, the film shows how his friends were in a state of panic, some were mourning and others were terrified....There was one scene that I thought was rather interesting.....St Veronica, as we all know is the person noted in Scripture who wiped the face of Christ as he carried his cross......In Gibson's film, Veronica was perfectly at peace almost like she knew the outcome of Jesus rising from the dead before it happened...In fact, she even was courageous in the face of all the madness going on around her.......Mel Gibson in this film gave St Veronica an insight the first disciples did not have....Veronica knew who Jesus really was, that he was God and that death had no power over him....Why bring this up?...Because today we hear the words from St John the Baptist......He tells us to prepare for the coming of Christ.....St Veronica was prepared - Are we prepared?.....Or maybe a better question is.....How do we prepare?....The Season of Advent gives Catholics roughly 30 days to pray, fast and give alms in order to prepare our hearts for the birth of Christ...Advent is also a time to make a good Sacramental Confession....This is how we prepare for the coming of God...St Veronica in the film was at peace as the world around her was crumbling...The only way to acquire peace in such circumstances is if our hearts are "right with God".....Only grace can give us that kind of "unshakeable peace" when we are living through the "storms of life" and when we face death, our death or the death of a loved one

"Those who sow in tears shall reap rejoicing"

Today in the second reading from Mass...St Paul to reminds us about this theme of preparation...."I am confident of this, that the one who began a good work in you will continue to complete it until the day of Christ Jesus".......Paul in making this statement to his friends is encouraging them....As my father would always say to me..."Joe - Straight ahead".....At our Baptism, the seed of faith was implanted into our hearts......It is now for us to nurture that seed and if we do, it will grow....."The kingdom of heaven is like a mustard seed that a person took and sowed in a field. It is the smallest of all the seeds, yet when full-grown it is the largest of plants. It becomes a large bush, and the 'birds of the sky come and dwell in its branches".....Like St Veronica in Mel Gibson's movie The Passion of the Christ...She understood what was going on around her, even when everyone else was panicking...St Veronica had "vision" - She understood that Jesus was born to die, so that we can one day live forever......."Do not let your hearts be troubled. You have faith in God; have faith also in me. In my Father's house there are many dwelling places. If there were not, would I have told you that I am going to prepare a place for you? And if I go and prepare a place for you, I will come back again and take you to myself, so that where I am you also may be. Where I am going you know the way"......Are we prepared?......Ready or not......Here I come

PERSONAL NOTES:

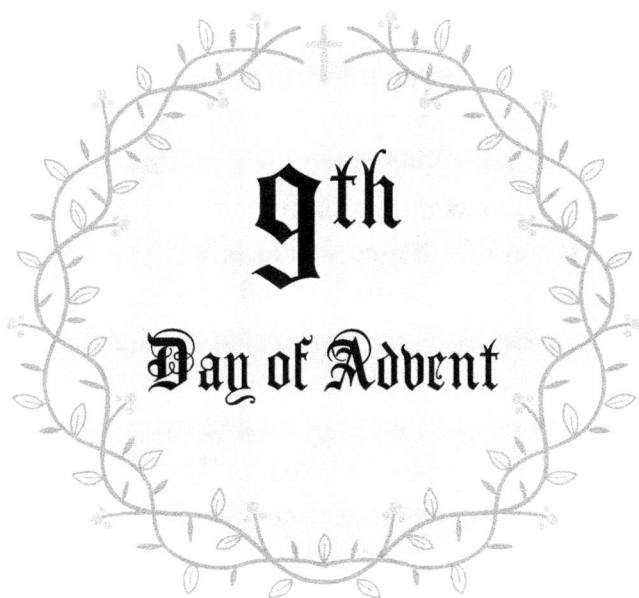

9th
Day of Advent

WHAT IS HOLDING YOU BACK?....
"FOR NOTHING IS IMPOSSIBLE
WITH GOD"

Today the Universal Church celebrates the Solemnity of the Immaculate Conception ..Mary was conceived free from sin unlike us because she was called to bear the son of God ..Jesus who also was pure could not come from something that was stained by sin - Think about it Therefore God preserved Mary from original sin by the merits of his son .. William Wordsworth called Mary "our tainted natures solitary boast" ..For this reason she is mankind's hope that one day we to will ascend into heaven body & soul .In the mean time Mary intercedes for us with her son ..Because no one knows the son as does the Mother .Mary is our Mother too Jesus gave her to us from the Cross "When Jesus saw his mother and the disciple there whom he loved, he said to his mother, "Woman, behold, your son." Then he said to the disciple, "Behold, your mother." And from that hour the disciple took her into his home" ..The most direct path to Jesus is through Mary . As all good mothers She takes us my the hand and shows us the way to her beloved son ."His mother said to the servers, "Do whatever he tells you" That could be the best advice ever given "Do whatever he tells you"

"The LORD has made his salvation known: in the sight of the nations he has revealed his justice. He has remembered his kindness and his faithfulness toward the house of Israel"

Today at Holy Mass we hear from St Luke the story of the Annunciation......"Do not be afraid, Mary, for you have found favor with God. Behold, you will conceive in your womb and bear a son, and you shall name him Jesus".....When we read scripture its very easy to forget that Mary was a historical figure as well as a biblical figure.......That means she was as real as we are......And Scripture today tells us she was afraid at what was being asked of her by God...That is a very human response....Following the Lord is not an easy task at times...God asks us to do things that appear to be impossible throughout the Gospel...However, God knows us better then we know ourself.......He knows what we are capable of - If only we trust him...This is why the archangel Gabriel says to Mary, "Do not be afraid"......Have you ever been faced with something that you think to be impossible?........Well, it does not get more impossible than a virgin to have a child...But again, the angel addresses that in the gospel today as well...."And the angel said to her in reply, "The Holy Spirit will come upon you, and the power of the Most High will overshadow you. Therefore the child to be born will be called holy, the Son of God. And behold, Elizabeth, your relative, has also conceived a son in her old age, and this is the sixth month for her who was called barren; for nothing will be impossible for God"......Do you think God's hand only reaches out to Mary and not to you as well?...God can do the impossible for you too - If you only give him your YES as Mary did......As Catholics when we get married we are called to be open to life...That means never using contraception.....To say that you never use contraception in this day and age is thought to be crazy...But this is what the church teaches and inorder for your marriage to be Sacramental, which means God's grace is acting in and through it, a Catholic couple must always be open to life never to use contraception.....Now don't shoot the messenger...I am not making this up...I am only telling you what the Church teaches....My wife and I have been married for 11 years...We have never used contraception…..My wife has given birth to 5 children….What people may not know is, we have also conceived and lost 3 children as well…..I have not told many people this but two months ago, my wife Sabryna was pregnant again for the eighth time……For just one week, we thought we were going to have another baby…. How I found out was, I found my wife crying on our bed…She was terrified because she has had 5 c-sections and after the last child the doctor told us that having another baby could be hazardous to my wife's health…..After she and I spoke, we called our doctor…. My wife's body does not produce enough progesterone naturally and that is why we lost two other children in the past….The doctor immediately prescribed progesterone shots to help keep the baby alive in her womb……….We only went through one cycle of the shots before we lost the child…Our third child lost over the course of eleven years of marriage…..For one week, we anticipated another baby coming into our home…..Why tell you this?…Because my wife while open to life (and still is) was terrified when she thought she was having another child because she was told after five c-sections her life would be in danger…Yet, she trusted God and still does!…Why?…..Because God always takes care of his children and God does not give us something to do that cannot be done, if we trust him - Take that to the bank!…."For nothing is impossible with God".

"Hail, Mary, full of grace, the Lord is with you; blessed are you among women"

Scripture tells us that Mary was afraid….But she got beyond her fear and put her hand into the hand of God….We must do the same…..Following God is not always easy….But I am fully convinced its the only way to live…A life filled with God's grace can do all things….As married couples we need God's grace and God will never let us down……..But we need to learn to trust him…. As St Luke's gospel today tells us…Mary said yes to the angel even though she was afraid……"Mary said, "Behold, I am the handmaid of the Lord. May it be done to me according to your word." Then the angel departed from her"…..As children of Mary we too must learn to trust and be open to God with a true and clean heart - And if we do, the "Holy Spirit will come upon you" too……What is holding you back?….."For nothing is impossible with God"

PERSONAL NOTES:

10th
Day of Advent

ARE YOU WILLING TO LEAVE THE
99 TO CHASE AFTER THE ONE WHO
IS LOST?.....THERE IS A COST - BE
WILLING TO PAY IT

Today at Holy Mass we hear from St Matthew's Gospel Jesus tells his friends something that sounds very good on paper and most would agree with it but when it translates into real time, the "good" people who are "left" behind usually get upset .We see this today in the Church ."If a man has a hundred sheep and one of them goes astray, will he not leave the ninety-nine in the hills and go in search of the stray? And if he finds it, amen, I say to you, he rejoices more over it than over the ninety-nine that did not stray. In just the same way, it is not the will of your heavenly Father that one of these little ones be lost" The Pontificate of Pope Francis has been very controversial ..We can disagree with his methods and style (I will publicly admit I do at times) but at the heart of his pontificate, whenever I read this text from St Matthew's Gospel I think of Pope Francis Many traditional Catholics have a big problem with Pope Francis .And frankly, I will also publicly admit, I believe they do not understand him (He can be hard to read) ..The root of this misunderstanding comes from how Pope Francis "reaches his hands out" to those on the margins of society, public sinners far from God I will admit that I too question is approach at times as far as how he "reaches out" However, I do believe that Pope Francis in his heart, he is trying to help the lost And he is more than willing to leave the "99 in the hills" to go after the "one stray" .We can agree to disagree with how he sometimes does this, but we too should be willing to do the same ..The 99 already "get it" However, the one lost in "the wilderness" needs someone to "go the extra yard" to bring them back home That can be a messy process Did not Jesus do the same?

Jesus ate with public sinners as the "respectable people" spoke badly about him Jesus approached the woman at the well who was in an adulterous relationship - I am sure that did not go over too well either with the "respectable people" In following Jesus's instructions in the gospel today correctly, we must never water down the fullness of Church Teaching Why? Because we have no authority to do so ..However, we must ALWAYS be willing to "step out of our comfortable little box" and reach a hand to the "black sheep" who has gone astray ...Let the "respectable people" talk trash! .Jesus had a heart for sinners because he came to save sinners And so must we ...Why? ..Because we ourselves are sinners too!

"The day of the Lord is near; Behold, he comes to save us"

Having a big family with many children close in age can be challenging, especially when you take them to Mass....My wife and I do our best.....Once in awhile we get invited to event where many traditional (some call them orthodox) Catholics gather and usually there is a Mass along with the event...We have taken our family to these kinds of gatherings from time to time and when our kids (we have five, all of which are under 10 years old) act up, I will tell you, the looks my wife and I get from some of these "traditional" Catholics is far from being charitable.....When this happens, I take it in stride and offer it up...However, what consoles me is I think to myself of how Jesus would be so happy that my family is at Mass, even when the kids misbehave.....As for the people who have a problem with kids at Mass misbehaving...It seems to me, they are

"missing it".......Jesus was willing to jump into the "mix" of life...
And so must we...That can be very messy...Why?...Because life is
messy.....As Jesus taught his friend's today...We must be willing
to "leave the 99 to go after the one"....In doing that, the 99 may
get upset...Why?.....Because to do that "things get very messy" -
The "respectable" crowd may question your actions and challenge
your motives.....My advice today to you is - Let them talk their
trash!.....Like Jesus, who came for sinners, so must we...A father
loves all his children, the good and the bad alike...And if we do not
pursue the lost, how will they ever find there way back home?

*"They shall exult before the LORD, for he comes; for he comes
to rule the earth. He shall rule the world with justice and the
peoples with his constancy"*

In St Matthew's gospel today, Jesus was trying to teach his friends
that we must hate the sin but love the sinner...And to love the
sinner may mean we have to leave the "respectable" crowd in order
to reach a loving hand to the one who is lost.....In doing so, many
people will not understand....Many will challenge your actions...
And many will even speak badly of you...In response to those nega-
tive outcomes.....Jesus tells us very clearly in the Beatitudes (which
are the "blue print" to get us to heaven) how we are to think and to
accept the "cost" of discipleship..........."Blessed are you when they
insult you and persecute you and utter every kind of evil against you
falsely because of me. Rejoice and be glad, for your reward will be
great in heaven. Thus they persecuted the prophets who were before
you".....Are you willing to leave the 99 to chase after the one who
is lost?.....There is a cost - Be willing to pay it

PERSONAL NOTES:

11th
Day of Advent

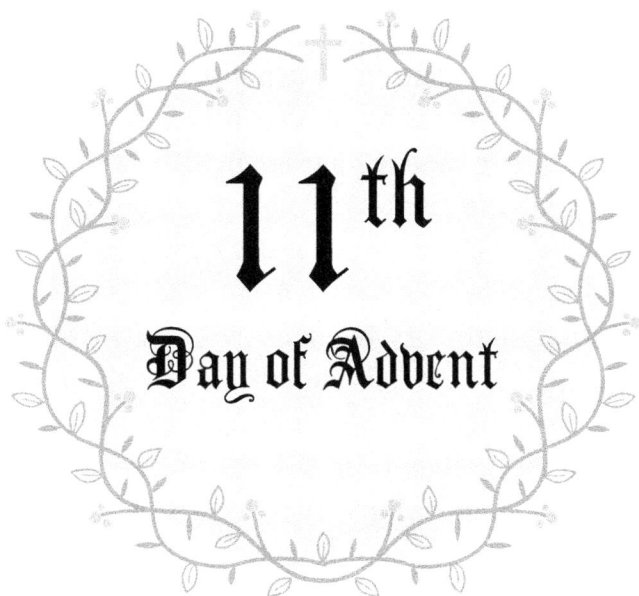

ITS EITHER ONE OR THE OTHER
MY FRIENDS...THE BURDEN OF SIN
OR THE BURDEN OF GOD'S WILL......
THERE IS NO ESCAPING THIS
CHOICE...SO CHOOSE WELL - A LOT
DEPENDS ON YOUR CHOICE

Today at Holy Mass we hear from St Matthew's gospel The text is very short but there are many layers to explore within it .."Jesus said to the crowds: "Come to me, all you who labor and are burdened, and I will give you rest. Take my yoke upon you and learn from me, for I am meek and humble of heart; and you will find rest for yourselves. For my yoke is easy, and my burden light" First question - Do you believe that the "yoke" of Christ is "easy and light"? . Let's be honest - Most do not ....Oh,how humanity gives lip service to God when it comes to doing what the Church says We somehow "think" its too much "It can't be done" ."Its not practical!"....Or we tell ourself ..If we attempt to do it, we will be "missing out" and will lead an incomplete life . Nothing could be further from the truth! God came to give us life and give it abundantly - That is in the here and now! When we come of age, we all make a choice and with that choice comes a "burden" - No getting around this reality! .If we choose the will of God, yes, there is a burden laid upon our shoulders But with that burden comes deep peace and joy .If we choose to ignore the will of God Some tell themselves that they will have it easier Actually, the very opposite happens Life becomes harder ..The burden of sin and death is infinitely heavier then the burden of the cross because with each choice we make there are consequences - No getting around it ..This is why Jesus tells us today .."For my yoke is easy, and my burden light" ..Its either one or the other The burden of sin or the burden of God's will ..There is no escaping this choice and no choice in and of itself is a choice ..Life with God is so much better then life without God

"Behold, the Lord comes to save his people; blessed are those prepared to meet him."

Words - Words - Words…So easily said…People need to see for themselves the truth of the Gospel…..Whenever I have a conversation with someone who "does not believe in God" or denies the Truth contained in the Catholic Church…I always point to this statement……….."You tell a tree by the fruit it bears"…When we look closely at the lives of people who follow the will of God and do not just give "lip service" to their Catholic faith…You will find they are joyful people, at peace with the world and with themselves, have stable marriages, they are self-disciplined, they are not enslaved by vices or debt…..Just open your eyes and take a good look……Now juxtapose that to the lives of people you know personally or who are apart of the mainstream culture who chose a lifestyle, which opposes God's will….Again, just open your eyes and take a good sober look……The outcome of the comparison should be obvious….But because the outcome of that comparison is so glaring…Mankind chooses not to "look" because if we did look and self-reflect, that would mean we would have to change….And there are many reasons why we do not want to change…The first of which is our pride………Many years ago I knew a man named Michael who had a long standing extra-marital affair…..After many years he came to terms with the pain he caused his wife and son and reconciled with the Church…I got to know Michael as he was healing…..I watched how God slowly healed his relationship with his wife…How God began working in Michael's life…..Now Michael is faithful Catholic…His marriage overtime has healed…. His son who was leading a bad life too has also started to pursue the Lord......All because Michael was willing to acknowledge his mistake, ask God to forgive him and rely on God's grace through daily prayer and the Sacraments to improve his marriage....As a result, Michael's life has drastically improved - Its as clear as the nose on your face!......Michael like many today could have given "lip service" to God (and to himself) and continued down the road he was on.....Lying to himself - "I'm doing just fine"......Instead, he was sick and tired of living the life he was living...He saw with his own two eyes the "good life", which is living in the state of grace and pursuing God's will......But here is the catch - There is always a catch...We cannot have it "both ways" - Far too many think we can...We cannot have God in our life and continue to pursue a life of sin....We must make a choice......Michael did and today Michael is a new man...His marriage is healed and he is thriving - Its as clear as the nose on your face!

> *"Come to me, all you who labor and are burdened, and I will give you rest. Take my yoke upon you and learn from me, for I am meek and humble of heart; and you will find rest for yourselves. For my yoke is easy, and my burden light"*

Today in the gospel, Jesus is telling us something that is universally true, no matter who we are....Life with God is infinitely better than life without God...The devil tries to tell humanity otherwise - And far too many believe the lie - And make no mistake - It is a lie!.... The question is for all those reading this today - Do you believe me?....If you don't, this is what I have to say to you - "You tell a tree by the fruit it bears"...All you have to do is take a good sober look.....Living in and through the will of God works...Such a life brings deep peace and it brings joy.....Still don't believe me?.... Why don't you take another look?....If you do, maybe just maybe you will then "take the first step" and make a change?........Its either one or the other my friends…The burden of sin or the burden of God's will…..There is no escaping this choice…So choose well - A lot depends on your choice

PERSONAL NOTES:

12ᵗʰ
Day of Advent

ITS THE SMALL THINGS IN LIFE
THAT MAKE LIFE BEAUTIFUL....
AND MORE TIMES THEN NOT, GOD
SPEAKS TO US THROUGH THE
SMALL THINGS....DO YOU NOTICE
THE SMALL THINGS?

Today the Universal Church celebrates the Feast of Our Lady of Guadalupe For those who are not familiar .In December of 1531, Mary appeared to a man named Juan Diego, a Mexican Indian requesting that a Church be built When Juan Diego brought this message to his bishop, the bishop was not convinced .Until Juan Diego returned with his cloak full of roses, which do not grow in December and when those same roses dropped from his cloak, Our Lady's image appeared on the cloak miraculously This same cloak with the image of Mary can be viewed to this day in the Cathedral, which was built as Our Lady requested in Mexico City That same Church is visited by more people throughout the world, only second to St Peter's Basilica in Rome .Why is all this important? The message Juan Diego brought to the bishop was something most if not all of us would not believe if he told it to us in real time as it happened Yet, what was asked by Our Lady, that a church be built happened! .What can we learn from this? God's ways are not our ways! With that said and something to keep in mind Mankind can not thwart the plans of God! Oh, how we think we can But its like trying to hold back the ocean .Those who fight against God are fighting a losing battle, both in the world and within themselves In the Book of Revelation, which was written by St John - When Mary gave birth to the Child Jesus - This is what John wrote ."Then I heard a loud voice in heaven say: "Now have salvation and power come, and the Kingdom of our God and the authority of his Anointed" ..The world 2000 years ago saw a child born in a barn - But God in heaven saw something else What do you see? I will tell you what I see - What is to be revealed will be like nothing the

world has ever seen! ."A great sign appeared in the sky, a woman clothed with the sun, with the moon under her feet, and on her head a crown of twelve stars"

"The angel Gabriel was sent from God to a town of Galilee called Nazareth, to a virgin betrothed to a man named Joseph, of the house of David, and the virgin's name was Mary"

The "language of God" is very different then the language of man.....What do I mean by that?....God uses events and people that the world seems to always miss....The message of Our Lady of Guadalupe was given to a poor Mexican Indian.....St Peter was the first Pope and he was a humble fisherman....The children of Fatima were poor peasants......To name a few examples.....And lastly Jesus, the King of King was born in a barn to humble parents... It always seems that while the world is looking for "extravagant signs"...God sends us messages and messengers, who are far from extravagant...And because they are not "flashy" we ignore them or miss the message....So the question is...How can we become receptive to the messages of God?......The answer to that question does not come from a persons resume or intellect...It comes from the purity of heart of that individual...Our Lady spoke to the children of Fatima and gave them one of the most important messages since the birth of Christ...Would you give such a message to children?...I will answer that question for you - I would not.... And a better question...Would you have believed the children of Fatima in real time if they told you they saw and spoke with "a beautiful lady"?…Again, I will answer for you - I probably would not have believed them…So how do we purify our hearts?……Jesus instructs us in Scripture…."Amen, I say to you, unless you turn and become like children, you will not enter the kingdom of heaven. Whoever humbles himself like this child is the greatest in the kingdom of heaven"…Jesus did not say, the people who graduate from Harvard will enter the Kingdom of God..He said we must become like children, who have pure and trusting hearts…The world has a way to make our hearts jaded and cynical…We all have "seen too much"…We have been disappointed by people…We have been hurt…..While this is true…Only God can heal our hearts and keep them pure…Only God!……Our world today thirsts for sophistication….God thirsts for us to remain pure, like a child…To look with wonder at everyday things and events….To trust…My youngest child is three years old…When I pick Maria up from Pre-K3, when she sees me, she runs with open arms directly at me…When I pick her up, Maria always places her face up against my cheek and keeps it there….Maria is so precious and so pure - Its tangible…..This is how we must strive to be….A person who is a "pure drop of water in the world" can do more than 100 people with Ivy league degrees!….God continues to "write his story" with and through the small and the pure of heart in the world…..And if we do not look with "eyes wide open", we will miss it

"The LORD will possess Judah as his portion in the holy land, and he will again choose Jerusalem. Silence, all mankind, in the presence of the LORD! For he stirs forth from his holy dwelling"

The Feast of Feast of Our Lady of Guadalupe should be a reminder to us of what God values….God is not interested in our resume… He is interested in our heart…We must learn to value the "things of God"…Because the "things of God" are very different from what are valuable to the world…..Why is this important?…Because if we do not value what is important to God, we will miss his message of Salvation…We will miss the guidance God provides to us day in and day out…..Only when our hearts become "childlike" will we "hear" this message…Like my three year old daughter Maria…. Who is so pure of heart and trusting….When she presses her cheek up against my face…As her Dad, I get a small taste of heaven here on earth each and everyday…..Its the small things in life that make life beautiful…And more times then not, God speaks to us through the small things….Do you notice the small things?

PERSONAL NOTES:

13th
Day of Advent

THIS IS THE TASK AT HAND...."IF TODAY YOU HEAR HIS VOICE, HARDEN NOT YOUR HEARTS"

Today at Holy Mass we hear in the gospel of St Matthew how Jesus tells the crowd that no matter who God sends to the people, they simply do not want to hear it .."To what shall I compare this generation? It is like children who sit in marketplaces and call to one another, 'We played the flute for you, but you did not dance, we sang a dirge but you did not mourn.' For John came neither eating nor drinking, and they said, 'He is possessed by a demon.' The Son of Man came eating and drinking and they said, 'Look, he is a glutton and a drunkard, a friend of tax collectors and sinners.' But wisdom is vindicated by her works" What should this tell us? .The problem is not the message or even the messenger The problem seems to be the hardness of our hearts .Mankind just does not want to hear it because mankind does not want to change ..We would rather wallow in your own misery than admit we were wrong and work to make a change .This my friends is a BIG problem as well as a BIG obstacle to overcome .. In order for us to enter heaven, we must "get past" this mindset .As life moves on many things begin to "breakdown" Our bodies become weaker Our mind is not as sharp Our career prospects are not as numerous As we see and feel our own mortality we should reflect more upon how our time here on earth really does end! But life does not have "end" with our mortal death But that outcome is entirely up to us! ..We must make a choice and no choice is a choice We will surely die one day and getting into heaven is not a "given" Its a choice, a daily one and that choice begins now "If today you hear his voice, harden not your hearts"

"The Lord will come; go out to meet him! He is the prince of peace"

The human mind is a funny thing….On paper something can be perfectly logical, like a mathematical solution, yet the human mind will look at the solution and swear up and down that the right answer is not the right answer…Even at the cost of personal pain and hardship as a result of questioning the right answer……As I have stated before in these reflections…"You tell a tree by the fruit it bears" and if the world was perfectly logical and open to correction, the world would make the necessary changes to "bear fruit"… But that is not how it works sadly…..The good news is God does not give up on us…God knows us better then we know ourselves and as a result, he puts in front of us people and situations in life to help us to "see"….That is what life really is all about…We are all on a journey back to God but in order to get to our final destination, we must be purified….We can resist that "process" and most do to a certain degree…But as we get older we "should" start to see that the "process" is for our own good…But as with all things, "the process" of us "figuring it out" comes to an end when we die…..When we face God and we all will - God will show us how he continuously reached a hand out to us throughout our entire life…God does that in so many different ways…But then it is up to us to reach a hand back!…If we choose not to - How can we expect to enter the Kingdom of Heaven?…….Life around us changes all the time and we must change as well…..St Paul tell us in Scripture…."When I was a child, I used to talk as a child, think as a child, reason as a child; when I became a man, I put aside childish things"…In

telling us that, St Paul is implying we must constantly "evolve"...
Only to become the people God created us to be, a holy people,
ready to enter the Kingdom of God........This "process" applies to
all of us...I distinctly remember when Pope John Paul II died...He
was completely broken and old...This man at one time was athletic,
a great communicator and had a brilliant mind - He had it all!...
Then age set in and God slowly "took everything away"...Some
may say that was unfortunate...And from a worldly prospective it
was sad to see...But if we "look underneath the surface"...God was
"stripping away" all Pope John Paul's gifts for a reason....Leaving
him with nothing more than God himself....This is how it all began
and how it all ends for all of us - For the great and the small of the
world alike...To view life in this manner and accept it...To accept
what God gives and takes away...All of which is apart of the sanctification process....Whether we accept this reality or not is up to
us...Not accepting it however does not change it - Get that though
your head!...In not accepting it we just become bitter...But if we
accept the "process of sanctification", when presented to us through
the events and outcomes of life...Life is so much more enjoyable
- We have peace - We have a purpose - And we see clearly our
destination in the distance...All this requires us to overcome our
greatest obstacle...The hardness of our hearts....Remember what
Jesus said in the gospel today at Mass...."Wisdom is vindicated by
her works"......The outcomes of our choices in the here and now
should tell us "what works and what does not work"...Its then up
to us to be honest with ourselves and make changes

"If today you hear his voice, harden not your hearts"

Today in St Matthew's Gospel Jesus addresses the crowd who
rejects him.....His statement gets "underneath" all the excuses the
people give for not listening to God...A good priest once told me

something I will never for get…He said, "Joe, many people will tell you all the reasons why they do not like the Catholic Church, why they will never go back to Church or why they will never be Catholic…But under all those reasons…There is one big reason and that reason is not communicated……And that obstacle to God is very real, very personal and many times very painful…..This is our task as Catholics, to help the world "get over" that one big "obstacle", which keeps them from God…How do we do this?…….We do this by our witness not by our words…And in order to give such a witness, we must strive to become a holy people…This is the task at hand…."If today you hear his voice, harden not your hearts"

PERSONAL NOTES:

14th

Day of Advent

"IT TAKES US TO FIRST RECOGNIZE
OUR OWN POVERTY BEFORE WE CAN
RECOGNIZE JESUS'S DIVINITY"

Today at Holy Mass we hear from the gospel of St Matthew Jesus friends ask him a question ."Why do the scribes say that Elijah must come first?" He said in reply, "Elijah will indeed come and restore all things; but I tell you that Elijah has already come, and they did not recognize him" .As many know, Elijah was a great prophet. Scripture tells us "There appeared the prophet Elijah whose words were as a flaming furnace. Their staff of bread he shattered, in his zeal he reduced them to straits; By the Lord's word he shut up the heavens and three times brought down fire" .Yet, according to Jesus told to us at Mass today, "They did nor recognize him" ..Early this week on the Feast Day of Our Lady of Guadalupe, I wrote about how God works through little children and the "invisible segments of society" more times then not Here again Jesus tells us A great message was given to the people and they did not hear it .So it is today as it was 2000 years ago - Not much has changed ..The message of Salvation is being proclaimed today at every Mass offered all over the world .We are given the privilege of receiving the Blessed Sacrament into our very body .We are given the opportunity to have our sins forgiven in the Sacrament of Reconciliation Yet, as it was in the time of Elijah "The people did not recognize him"

"Lord, make us turn to you; let us see your face and we shall be saved"

How can we recognize Christ in our world today?…..A question often asked by many…More time then not, it takes us to first recognize our own poverty before we can recognize Jesus's divinity… That is a lofty statement - I am going to say it again….."It takes us to first recognize our own poverty before we can recognize Jesus's divinity"…Let me try to explain it…..Being citizens of America for the most part all our basic needs at met….We all eat well, we have a roof over our head, cloths on our back……In many cases we have deposable income……We are in good health…All these things are good, however in having them the way we do in abundance, we can "think" we do not need God….Sometimes it takes an event to make us feel utterly powerless - Its then, in such a moment like that will we be open to really "listen" to what God is trying to tell us….. While we all want to achieve some level of material comfort, being too comfortable in this life can be a distraction for us when it comes to "seeing and hearing" God in the hear and now……Having money is not a sin…I will admit to you right now…My wife and I are professional people and we are hardly poor…I would be lying to you if I told you otherwise…However, my wife and I have five children…We use the material gifts given to us and share them with our family and put them at the service of the world….…...This is what the Social Compendium of the Catholic Church says about wealth…."Wealth is considered a gift from God that should be used responsibly and shared with those in need, meaning that accumulating excessive wealth while others lack basic necessities is morally wrong; individuals have a duty to use their wealth to benefit society and not just hoard it for personal gain"….As an American , hearing this is challenging because our culture is so driven by material goals and achievements - Its pounded into our heads as children - "Get a good job and make tons of money!"…What the Church is teaching us in this document is the following…Money is not a bad thing…

We are to work hard and reach our potential and that may mean a significant amount of material success will be gained...However, what the Church is also telling us is....If we are gifted with material wealth, its for us to use that wealth for the benefit of the Kingdom of God.....Why?....Because if we look to "build heaven on earth", we will get distracted and not look to God...We will "think" we do not need him.....Also, our true home is heaven....And if we try to find "heaven on earth" not only will we always be disappointed because nothing fully satisfies us materially speaking in the here and now no matter how good it is, but if we live for material gain, we will ultimately find ourselves constantly violating the first and second commandments...To love God above all things and love your neighbor as yourself

"To whom much is given, much will be required"

Today at Mass Jesus tells his friends that a message was given to the world and the world did not hear it....As Catholics, everything we need to hear is written down very clearly for us...Its for us to read it and put it into practice...So here is the final question - Why do we ignore what is told to us? - The answer can be found in this state-ment - Because we "think" we do not need God...We get distracted by our creature comforts more often then not...Only and until we recognize our own poverty before God, even if we are blessed with material wealth, will we have "eyes to see" and "hears to hear"....As Catholics, wealth is seen as a stewardship, meaning individuals are entrusted with managing their riches for the good of others, not just themselves.......I can hear it now..."Your a communist Joe"!........ No - I'm a Catholic - And "My kingdom is not of this world"..."To whom much is given, much will be required"

PERSONAL NOTES:

15th

Day of Advent

ANY MORE QUESTIONS OUT
THERE?.....ITS REALLY PLAIN
AND SIMPLE.......JESUS WAS A
CARPENTER NOT A PHYSICIST....
WE NEED TO STOP MAKING THINGS
THAT ARE NOT COMPLICATED SO
COMPLICATED

Today at Holy Mass we hear from the gospel of St Luke The people are coming to John the Baptist and asking him for advice ."What should we do?" What John tells them frankly is very practical, its not some esoteric soap-box litany of "things to do" .."Whoever has two cloaks should share with the person who has none. And whoever has food should do likewise. "Even tax collectors came to be baptized and they said to him, "Teacher, what should we do?" He answered them, "Stop collecting more than what is prescribed. "Soldiers also asked him, "And what is it that we should do?" He told them, "Do not practice extortion, do not falsely accuse anyone, and be satisfied with your wages" .And so it is to this very day 2000 years later .Doing the work of the Lord is written on the hearts of all men - Its very practical and frankly in many ways its straight up and down common sense Yet - We still inquire, like the people who approached John the Baptist - "What should we do?" Is it that we truly do not know what to do? ..Or .Is it we know what to do and do not want to do it? .We need to stop making things so complicated Jesus was a carpenter and his first disciples were fishermen ..What they taught was not "rocket-science" It all boils down to this - We are to love God above all things and love our neighbor as ourself And Jesus because he knows we are all flawed, gives us a Church, which gives us the Sacraments to help us to do the one thing he asks of us ..Anymore questions?

"Have no anxiety at all, but in everything, by prayer and petition, with thanksgiving, make your requests known to God."

I do not pay attention too much to Catholic Social Media even though I have a radio show, which airs primarily throughout Connecticut…Why you may ask?…Because many of the people heavy involved in Catholic Social Media, while in most cases these men and women are highly educated and very smart…..I find they focus on things that frankly would take care of themselves if their primary focus was to communicate First Principals….What do I mean by First Principals?……..Go to a Sacramental Confession once a month…Pray the Rosary with your family each day…..Fast every week……Make it a practice to go to Eucharistic Adoration on a weekly basis…Go to Mass daily (if you can) and Always receive the Eucharist in the state of grace…..These are First Principals…. Anyone can do them…And if we do them, everything else will fall into place….Why is that?…Because in doing these things, we will be given grace and everything relies upon grace…Also, in doing these things the Holy Spirit will dwell within our soul…And when the Holy Spirit finds a home within our soul we are given certain gifts…What are those gifts?……Wisdom, Understanding, Counsel, Fortitude, Knowledge, Piety, and Fear of the Lord……. Once we have these gifts…Everything will take care of itself… Speaking personally, my faith is grounded in First Principals…… Its not complicated…I try to keep it very simple…Why?…Because Jesus was not complicated…Jesus was a "blue-collar guy"…..He said things clearly and as Catholics we have everything written down, if we ever have any doubt about what the Church teaches and why it teaches what it teaches…Frankly, the rest is up to us…. So, stick with First Principals…….And if you do, I will bet the question asked today by the people to John the Baptist...."What should we do?".....Will no long be asked...Why?...Because the answer as far as "What should we do?" - Is written on the hearts of all men

"Then the peace of God that surpasses all understanding will guard your hearts and minds in Christ Jesus."

John the Baptist was a rough and tumble kind of guy...Like Jesus, he told it like it is.....The message of Salvation is very plain and very simple...You do not have to have a PhD to understand it, so in my opinion we should stop making things that are not complicated so complicated......We are to love God above all things and love our neighbor as ourself......And if we ground our Catholic faith in First Principals, we will execute on that one and only thing Jesus asks of us....Any more questions out there?.....Its really plain and simple.......Jesus was a carpenter not a physicist....We need to stop making things that are not complicated so complicated

PERSONAL NOTES:

16th

Day of Advent

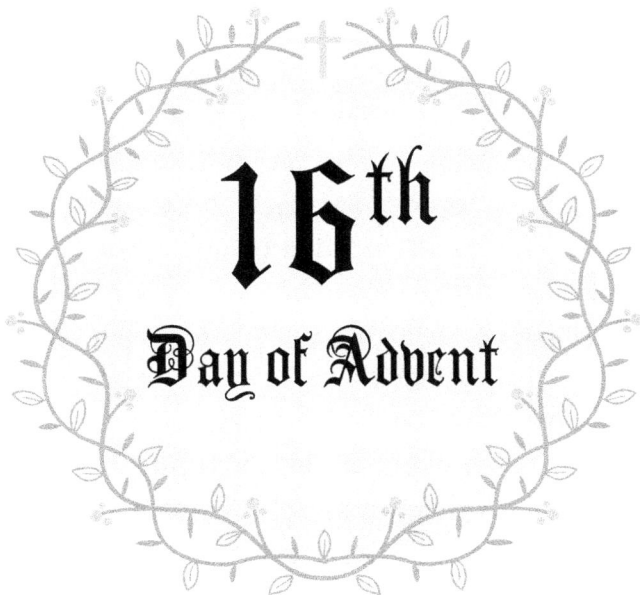

"I WILL TURN DARKNESS INTO LIGHT
BEFORE THEM, AND MAKE CROOKED
WAYS STRAIGHT. THESE ARE MY
PROMISES: I MADE THEM, I WILL NOT
FORSAKE THEM."

Today at Holy Mass we hear from the gospel of St Matthew ..In the text the teachers of the law question Jesus .."By what authority are you doing these things? . These men do not honor the Truth They honor power Not unlike the men and women of today .."Playing politics" results in everyone losing Yet, short term thinking continues to win the day .Building a life upon Truth requires a number of things .For one, it requires sacrifice and secondly, it requires something which was discussed in today's gospel ...."By what authority are you doing these things?" .We hear statements made today by very powerful people "This is my truth" ."That is your truth" ..How can there be a subjective truth? A life lived under the yoke of God is far better then a life lived under the yoke of power brokers of this earth, no matter what the political stripe they claim to be Yet, mankind is not convinced We continue to "play politics" and disregard the laws of God - To our own detriment .All because we do not want to "bend our knee" All because of our pride...All because we will not acknowledge that there is only one authority - God

"Your ways, O LORD, make known to me; teach me your paths, Guide me in your truth and teach me, for you are God my savior"

There is an old saying..."A man can not lead if a man does not know how to serve".....When a person acknowledges God and that God gave him his position of authority, then and only then will that man treat the people under him rightly....Without the grace of God and without God has the center of any power structure... In time, that power structure will eventually only serve a select few and disregard the needs of the masses.....History shows us this, yet mankind refuses to "see" it....All because mankind refuses to "bend its knee" to the God who loves him more then anyone could or ever will.........Years ago I used to volunteer with the Missionaries of Charity at an AIDS hospice on Saturdays in Lower Manhattan... The men who lived there were taken care of but as with any home, there were rules...No drinking or drugs, there was a curfew.....very basic things were asked of the men living there and if they followed the rules, they had a good life - Yet some men just could not or would not do it...Why?.....Because to accept rules means to accept authority and some people would rather "cut off their nose in spite of their face" before they accept someone telling them what to do.....There was this one man living in the house for a few months named Leroy...Leroy had AIDS and was a drug addict...For a time he was doing so good and before he was fully recovered from his addiction he asked to leave the home...The sister who was the superior at the time literally begged Leroy to stay - She knew he was not ready to leave yet - But Leroy was not having it, he wanted to do things his way...So Leroy left...Within three months we heard from the other men still living in the hospice that Leroy was found died in the Bronx.....Why tell you this story?.....All you have to do is look around and you do not have to look very far - How is "our way" working out?.....Jesus tells us in Scripture that I came to give you life and give it abundantly - That is in the here and now!... Yet we are not convinced!....We would rather "play politics".......We want to "do it our way" - Be damned the consequences or the personal costs.....It all comes down to the word authority - Do we acknowledge God as having it? - Or do we live in denial?.......At the end of the day - We cannot "save ourselves" nor do we go to heaven on "our terms"........There is a deep cost to pay for denying God's authority, at the end of our life and in the here and now as well...That is reality and reality does not change based upon - "My Truth"

> *"Good and upright is the LORD; thus he shows sinners the way. He guides the humble to justice, he teaches the humble his way."*

Today in the gospel from Mass Jesus's authority was questioned... And ironically enough, Jesus's authority is still questioned to this very day.....Mankind doubles-down and triples down on choices lived outside of God's law...Only to reap the consequences...And then mankind doubles and triples down again!.....Jesus tells us very clearly...."My yoke is easy and my burden is light, learn from me for I am meek and humble of heart"........Still not convinced?....God is our Father and God loves us.....A good father will never tell his children something that will hurt them.....We need to understand and more importantly feel the depths of God's love for us - Love changes everything - Not words but love put into action...If only we give God a chance, then maybe just maybe will we understand - The will of God was given to us for our own good.......In the mean time, God does not give up on us...Why? - Because he loves us..... "I will lay waste mountains and hills, all their undergrowth I will dry up; I will turn the rivers into marshes, and the marshes I will dry up. I will lead the blind on a way they do not know; by paths they do not know I will guide them. I will turn darkness into light before them, and make crooked ways straight. These are my promises: I made them, I will not forsake them."

PERSONAL NOTES:

17th

Day of Advent

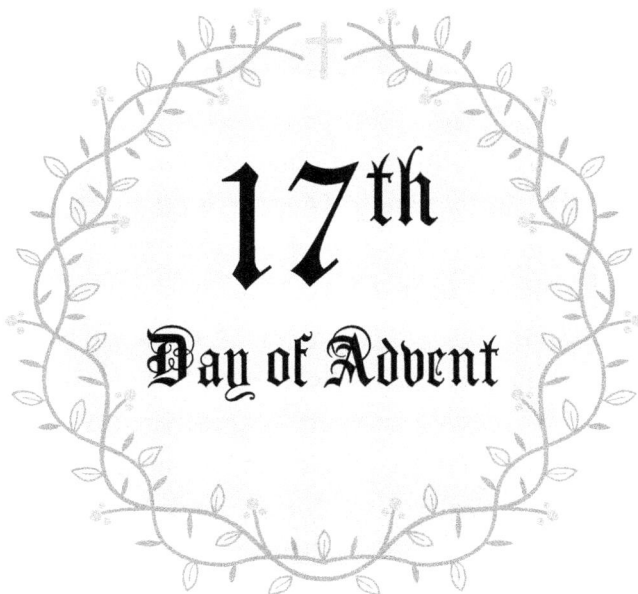

THIS IS HOW WE TRANSFORM THE
WORLD........ONE "PURE DROP OF
WATER" CAN DO MORE THEN 1000
GRADUATES FROM HARVARD OR
YALE...IF YOU ARE WHO YOU WERE
MEANT TO BE, YOU WILL SET THE
WORLD ON FIRE!

Today at Holy Mass we hear from the Gospel of St Matthew In this text Matthew writes about the genealogy of Jesus He notes "the total number of generations from Abraham to David is fourteen generations; from David to the Babylonian exile, fourteen generations; from the Babylonian exile to the Christ, fourteen generations" .While Jesus was God, he was also "fully man", born into a family, like all of us And as with every family, there are all kinds of people in it Saints and sinners alike I read a commentary this morning about this particular Gospel from a Trappist Monk This is what he said ."God creates and transforms from what he already created, he does not contradict himself, nor does he scrap everything at a troubled moment in order to start again "from scratch". His Son is born within time from a race of saints, sinners, ruffians, exiles, wisemen, poets, quarrelers" ..As it is with all of our families - What can we learn from this reality? That God works with and uses everyday and normal people God can transform a person into his instrument, which will produce an enormous amount of good in the world I don't think we believe that! - Why? .Because we allow the world to "label us" To "limit" us And we believe the lie too! All you have to do is read the lives of the saints They were no different then you .The Council of Vatican II wrote about what is commonly referred to in Catholic circles as the universal call to holiness ..That means, not just the clergy can become holy Holiness is for everyone and it is possible We have been given as Catholics all the tools we need by the Catholic Church to become a holy people And sadly, most people do not utilize these tools nor do we prioritize this goal - To become holy ..I

will publicly state this right now There is no greater goal to strive for on this earth than to become a holy person .There is no greater achievement! ..Why? Because one "pure drop of water" can do more than 1000 graduates from Harvard or Yale God can transform the ordinary into the extraordinary Why should we settle for the ordinary?

"O Wisdom of our God Most High, guiding creation with power and love: come to teach us the path of knowledge!"

If you have ever met someone who was truly holy, you will remember that person for the rest of your life…I have been blessed to have encountered many holy people…Most of them were nuns… But I have also met many selfless "regular people", like you and me, who have witnessed these holy nuns and in turn gave their lives to serving their fellow men and women…There is power contained in a holy life - Such a witness is contagious - Saints make other saints!….When a person sees for themself what holiness really looks like…A person will want that "something" and ask, "Why can't I be like that too?"……..When I was going to India to serve with Mother Teresa's sisters every December I met a lot of interesting people from around the world…One of those people was a retired nurse from Bologna, Italy named Teresa…Teresa never married and when she retired in her fifties she traveled to Kolkata to meet Mother Teresa….When she met Mother Teresa, Mother Teresa told Teresa from Italy, we need you to stay in Kolkata!….How does one respond to such a bold request from a world famous saint?….

So Teresa, the retired nurse from Bologna, Italy spent 30 years of her retirement (spending 8 months of each year) in Kolkata India serving along side Mother Teresa's sisters...I met Teresa when she was very old.....One year we both rented rooms in a Church not far from the Missionaries of Charity Convent .....Mass was always at 6:00am...At 5:00am, I would smell Teresa making Italian coffee before Mass..She was an old woman at this point - I always admired how brave she was - She traveled to India all alone.....Teresa, the simple retired nurse encountered Mother Teresa...And that one encounter propelled her to become a holy person...Because saints make other saints!...The last year I was in India and saw Teresa we were both working at the Home for the Dying and the Destitute... One morning, a poor street woman came into the home ready to have a baby - The woman was heavily pregnant....Teresa the nurse from Bologna Italy, who was almost 80 years old delivered the baby all by herself - No doctor needed!...... This story is another example of God taking an "average person" and transforming them into something they never thought possible.....Because to become holy is possible...Its the greatest thing you can do while you walk this earth....It is something we were ALL created to become - A holy people!......This is how we transform the world........One "pure drop of water" can do more then 1000 graduates from Harvard or Yale...If you are who you were meant to be, you will set the world on fire!

"Justice shall flourish in his time, and fullness of peace for ever"

Today's gospel from Mass tells us a little bit about the family of Jesus...How his family was far from perfect....Just like all of our families...However from that very "normal" family came the savior of the world...Now, none of us are called to save the world

- That job has been taken, however, each of us are called to become holy and a holy life is within the grasp of every person - We each have something very special to do!........Like anything else in life, you have to really want it!...You need to make it your life's priority...And if you make this decision....If you strive to follow the Carpenter from Nazareth with reckless abandon...Trust me when I tell you this....Your life's example will set the world around you on fire!...Don't believe me?...Just ask a simple retired nurse from Bologna Italy....One encounter with a holy person changed the direction of her life forever...She was transformed...And the rest is history....This is how we transform the world........One "pure drop of water" can do more then 1000 graduates from Harvard or Yale... If you are who you were meant to be, you will set the world on fire!

PERSONAL NOTES:

18th
Day of Advent

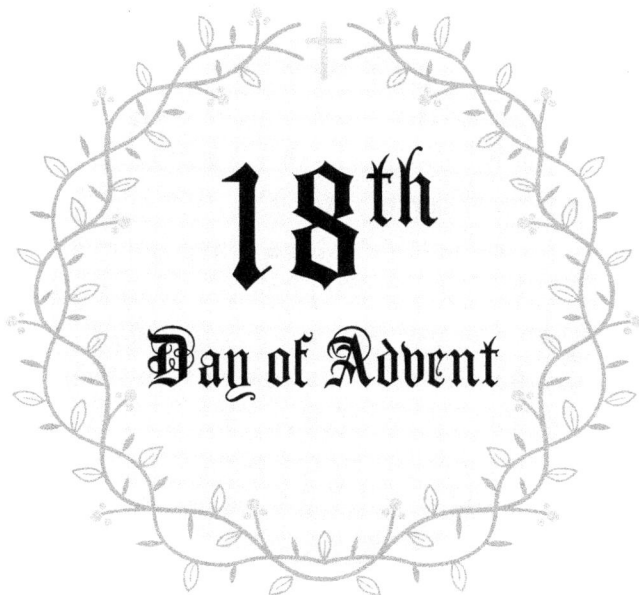

REMEMBER, WE ARE ALL
"PRACTICING CATHOLICS", WHICH
IMPLIES WE NEED TO "PRACTICE"
BECAUSE "PRACTICE MAKES
PERFECT"

Today at Holy Mass we hear from the Gospel of St Matthew The text today focuses on St Joseph, the foster father of Jesus and the husband of Mary .Joseph was a "regular guy". However Joseph's faith was iron-clad .He took God at his word .And was obedient even when things did not make sense Joseph played the "long-game" Even when he could not "see" the end result .Joseph trusted that God could and that God's plan was far greater than his own ."Joseph, son of David, do not be afraid to take Mary your wife into your home. For it is through the Holy Spirit that this child has been conceived in her. She will bear a son and you are to name him Jesus, because he will save his people from their sins" ..So the question is How do we acquire faith like St Joseph? Like anything else, we work at it! The term "Practicing-Catholic" should tell us everything we need to know When we "practice" at something, this implies we are not perfect No one is perfect - That is why we practice ..The more we purify our hearts, through the Sacramental life, through daily prayer, through weekly fasting, through living a sacrificial life serving our families God will give us grace And the result of that grace will strengthen our faith The problem is We sell ourselves too short! ..We are ALL capable of accomplishing things that are far beyond our wildest imagination! ..We simply must put our hand into the hand of God and never look back! ..Because God sees the entire picture, we do not .In order to trust in this manner requires us to "practice" our Catholic faith .And as any athlete knows   .."Practice makes Perfect"

"When Joseph awoke, he did as the angel of the Lord had commanded him and took his wife into his home"

All great things start small…A priest told me once, "Joe - Every great business at one time started out in a garage"……If we use this analogy, we can say the same thing about ourselves….We are all a work in progress - When God looks at us, he sees nothing but potential…..We are the ones that sell ourselves short and believe the lie of the evil one - "You can't do that!"……Tell the devil to go to hell!…….Before we can believe in ourselves the way that God does, we must allow "the seed" of faith to germinate and grow……That is really our one and only job - To do all the things to make our faith grow….Simple things that really do not take too much time…Pray the Rosary every day, Go to a Sacramental Confession once a month….Let me stop there…Do you really think that what you have done in your life God has not heard or seen before?…Do you really think the priest hearing confession has never heard sins like yours before?….Time to get over it and take the step!…….Let me continue…Receive the Blessed Sacrament in the state of grace weekly…Fast on Friday…..Siting before the Blessed Sacrament once a week in silence for 15 minutes……If we do these simple things that cost nothing, in time….The "seed" of faith placed in us at baptism will GROW!!!…That is all we have to do and God will do the rest…..The "fruit" that will come from those activities are limitless!!!…Don't believe me?…Look at St Joseph…He was just a "regular guy"…Look at what God accomplished through him…. Please allow me tell you about another "regular person" who let God work through them……Many years ago I found myself on a connecting flight from New Delhi to Kolkata…It was a small commercial flight leaving at night…Most of the people on the plane were locals from the West Bengal State of India…By this time I was a seasoned traveller through this part of the world, so I could identify by sight what people from Eastern India looked like and the language they spoke....Interestingly enough on the plane sitting directly behind me was an Afro-American woman with a Southern accent...We were the only two Americans on the plane and as you could imagine, we both "stuck-out" like sore thumbs....So I started talking to this woman…......"What are you doing here?"- I asked her...So she told me her story...She said she was from Houston Texas and her son died when he was a small child and the death of her son propelled her to fund and establish a school in Eastern India for poor children...She was on her way to visit the school.......Once again, I thought to myself...How brave this woman was - Her story left me speechless!...Traveling all by herself to a far corner of the world - She was not a young woman either!...Why bring this encounter up?......If you asked this lady, say thirty years ago - In your life you will establish a school and help thousands of children do you think she would have believed you? - Probably not...I got news for you! - If we trust God and allow our faith to grow - YOU may do even greater things than that!....... Scripture tells us….."If you have faith the size of a mustard seed, you would say to this mulberry tree, 'Be uprooted and planted in the sea,' and it would obey you"…..When we read that statement from the Bible we say to ourselves….."Whatever! - That can't be real"…..Tell that to the woman sitting next to me on the plane, that channeled the grief of losing a child into helping thousands of children and establishing a school against all odds! - She was just a "regular person"......God can do so much more with your life than you can do with it!....If only we allow the ever "small seed" of faith placed in us to grow

"Behold, the days are coming, says the LORD, when I will raise up a righteous shoot to David"

Today the gospel from Mass highlights the life of St Joseph…."A regular guy"……In St Joseph there was a complete submission to God's messenger and a total acceptance of the will of God…. Like with all things…"Rome was not built in a day"…St Joseph can serve as a model for us…..Remember, we are all "Practicing Catholics", which implies we need to "practice" because "practice makes perfect"

PERSONAL NOTES:

19th
Day of Advent

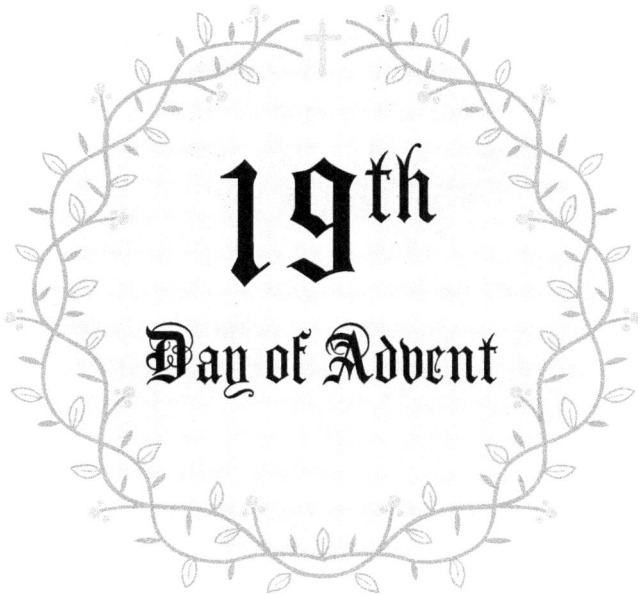

WORK WITH GOD NOT AGAINST
HIM...."HE HAS YOUR BACK" - AS
THE SAYING GOES IN MY PART OF
NEW JERSEY....HE IS CREATING A
MASTER PIECE AND THAT MASTER
PIECE IS YOU!!!

Today at Holy Mass we hear from the Gospel of St Luke .. The text tells us about the birth of John the Baptist How his parents, Zechariah and Elizabeth always wanted a child and could not conceive one ..At that time and in the culture in which Zechariah and Elizabeth lived, there was a stigma attached to not being able to have children Therefore Zechariah and Elizabeth had to live with a certain amount of shame ..Then out of nowhere, in her old age Elizabeth gets pregnant This is what she says ."So has the Lord done for me at a time when he has seen fit to take away my disgrace before others" ..Why did Elizabeth have to suffer unjustly for so long? ..This is a question we all can relate too ..God uses suffering more times then not to form us Its in times when we "go without", its in those times that God develops within us so many virtues And that is the name of the game To allow God to mold us .Create us to be an instrument of use for the Kingdom of God Speaking from personal experience That can be a painful process .But know this .I have learned to trust the process! And God is not done with me yet Nor is he done with YOU He loves us too much to leave us as we are

"For you are my hope, O LORD; my trust, O God, from my youth. On you I depend from birth; from my mother's womb you are my strength"

Years ago a friend of mine who was a priest would ask my wife and I to give talks to young married couples about to stand before

God and be joined together as husband and wife...The first thing I would ask these young men and women is this......"What is the goal of your marriage?".....Many of these couples were in their twenties and they would just look at me not knowing what to say...I would ask it again, because in many cases I knew what they were thinking......The goal of many American marriages is to live a comfortable life and retire after years of marriage with money in the bank staring at the ocean...While there is nothing wrong with being comfortable...That is not the goal of a Catholic marriage... The answer I was looking for was first for the young man to stand up and say..."My goal is to get my wife and children to heaven"... Next I wanted to hear his soon to be wife say..."My goal is to get my husband to heaven and my children as well"....BOOM!!!!... That is the answer!...And that is no small task in this day and age... Why bring this up now?.....In order for God to form us into the people we need to be....There needs to be changes made and some-times those changes can be painful...Trust me.....I am speaking from first hand experience here...But it is within those times that God forms us.....As Catholics we have all the "tools" to make this happen!......You see at the root of the problem, many in the world today do not view life as God views it....God only wants one thing - You in heaven!.....And many times because we have free will, we make choices that keep us from being the people we were born to be - A holy people...God will always respect our free will... However, God loves us too much to leave us in a condition, which prevents his grace from penetrating our hearts...So what does God do?.....He presents us with situations, which cause us to ques-tion our current state, with the goal of drawing us towards heav-enly things....When a young man discerns the priesthood or the married life, the best thing I heard about the discernment process is this...Follow your peace...God will not give you true peace if you choose something that keeps you from himself…So what does that mean for us now?…We must follow our hearts - Easier said than done - Right! - But we must do it…If we follow our heart, we will be given true peace and that is where we need to be!…….. There really is one goal in life…To allow God to sanctity us so we can enter heaven…..Think about this for a second…Most people want to "do good" in the world…..The closer we get to God on this earth, the more good we can do…First within our families then in the world around us…I wrote this yesterday in the morning reflection…A holy life is a powerful life!….However, to get to where we have to be can be a struggle….But God is the master builder… He knows what he is doing…Trust him!….."He takes away every branch in me that does not bear fruit, and every one that does he prunes so that it bears more fruit"……Just as a father when he looks at his 13 year old son…He knows how the "finished product" will look…God does the same thing with us…He is infinitely patient…His mercy is beyond all telling…And his grace is there for us to sustain us through it all!……Work with God, do not work against him…."He has your back" - As the saying goes in my part of New Jersey….He is creating a master piece and that master piece is YOU!!!

"O God, you have taught me from my youth, and till the present I proclaim your wondrous deeds"

The gospel today tells us about how it took along time for John the Baptist to be born….And once he was born…John lived in the desert…Only to be formed for a longer period of time…Until the time was right!…John the Baptist was the precursor to Christ…And as with everything in life - All good things take time…God formed John the Baptist to be the man he needed him to be…And John cooperated with the hand of God in that process of formation…

And look at the impact John had on the world....So it can be with us as well...We need to learn to cooperate with God....We are ALL the work of his hands....So if I was to ask you...Why were you born?...What is your purpose?......Like I would ask young Catholic couples about to get married...What is the purpose of your marriage?......This is what I want to hear...."My purpose is to allow God to form me to be the person I was born to be....And in doing so by my life's example, I will bring those around me to want and see the same thing for themselves"....This is what John the Baptist did...."I am not worthy to stoop and loosen the thongs of his sandals. I have baptized you with water; He will baptize you with the Holy Spirit".....Work with God not against him...."He has your back" - As the saying goes in my part of New Jersey....He is creating a master piece and that master piece is YOU!!!

PERSONAL NOTES:

20th
Day of Advent

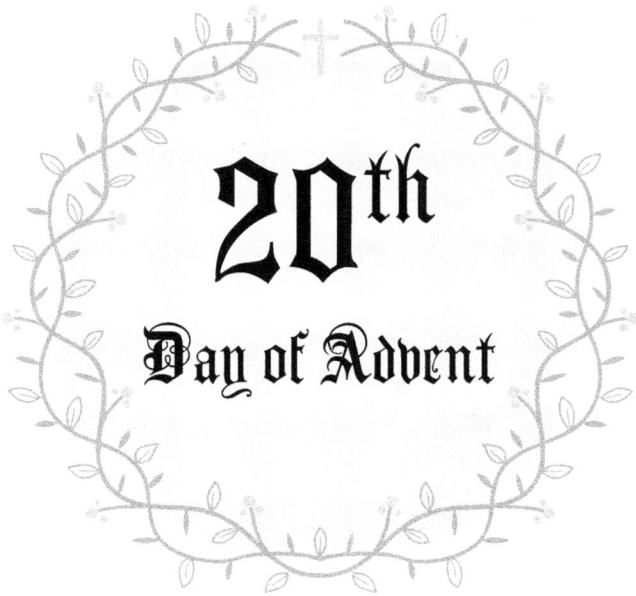

"MAY IT BE DONE TO ME ACCORDING TO YOUR WORD".....AT THE STATEMENT OF MARY THE GATES OF HELL TREMBLED!....AND WHEN WE SAY THAT STATEMENT TO THIS VERY DAY....THE GATES OF HELL TREMBLE ONCE AGAIN!

Today at Holy Mass we hear from the Gospel of St Luke . Mary is presented with the impossible "Behold, you will conceive in your womb and bear a son, and you shall name him Jesus" .As we all know, Mary was a virgin and having a baby as a virgin simply does not make any sense - Right?!? ..The angel Gabriel addresses that claim "The Holy Spirit will come upon you, and the power of the Most High will overshadow you. Therefore the child to be born will be called holy, the Son of God. And behold, Elizabeth, your relative, has also conceived a son in her old age, and this is the sixth month for her who was called barren; for nothing will be impossible for God" .So here is the question Do you really believe nothing is impossible for God? - Do we put God in a box, thinking he operates like we do? .God can do anything More importantly, God can use YOU to do the impossible .Our job is to respond like Mary did - With absolute trust ..Recognizing that without God we can do nothing but with God all things are possible

"Mary said, "Behold, I am the handmaid of the Lord. May it be done to me according to your word."

Those who know about Mother Teresa may not know that before she founded the Missionaries of Charity, Mother Teresa was a high school principal in an elite school for all girls in Kolkata...She served in that school for 20 years until God called her to work for the poorest of the poor in the streets...If you read about Mother Teresa's life, she would say that if she did not pick up the first

person she saw in gutter, the work that God called her to do would not have happened...It began with helping that first person......
All good things start small.......On one of my trips to Kolkata I visited a Leper Colony that Mother Teresa founded on the out-skirts of Kolkata - The Leper Colony is still there to this day...
Before Mother Teresa founded this home for lepers, people who contracted this disease literally were expelled from the city, young and old alike, left to die along the railroad tracks...No joke...So when Mother Teresa heard about the plight of those people, she went to help them with one other nun.....And under a tree, she began to distribute food and clothing.....Over time people heard about what this brave nun was doing and donations started to come in...All by the way unsolicited...Money just kept coming in.....
Why do I tell you this story?...When I visited this leper colony and was told how it started and how the project grew...All I could think to myself is HOW COULD THIS HAPPEN!....How could this huge village start from two nuns giving out food and clothing from under a tree...They did not even ask for money, yet people just donated tons of money...And with the funds, they gave the lepers of Kolkata dignity, a safe place to live, they created jobs for them so they could support their families...I simply could not believe how this could happen...Literally out of no where..........As I read the gospel this morning hearing what St Gabriel said....."For noth-ing will be impossible for God"...This story came to my mind.....
The Missionaries of Charity serve all over the world.....Feeding and caring for thousands upon thousands of people a day...I know because I have seen this with my own eyes...Did you know that the Missionaries of Charity NEVER solicit money - Never have...
That all the donations they get come in unsolicited - To this very day.....As a person who works in corporate America and has an MBA - Tell Mother Teresa "business model" to Harvard School

of Business…Allow me to "pitch it" right now….We are going to have 5000 nuns and around 100,000 lay volunteers all over the world….We are going to feed hundreds of thousand of people a day…..Without asking for one penny…And all the money we need is going to come in to address what we have to do without us asking for it….That is what Mother Teresa's "business model" looks like - No joke - And it works - To this day!….If I was to "pitch" that business model to a bank asking for a loan - What do you think the loan officer would say - Allow me to translate - BEAT IT!……Yet, this is how the Missionaries of Charity operate around the world…..How you may ask yourself?…….."For nothing will be impossible for God"

"He shall receive a blessing from the LORD, a reward from God his savior. Such is the race that seeks for him, that seeks the face of the God of Jacob."

Today we read in the gospel about the impossible…A virgin gives birth to a child…Many people in the world say - Whatever!….Did not happen!…..Or…….People read this story and say, "God can't work the impossible in my life"…….This is what I say to all the nay-sayers - WRONG! - God can do all things!…..I have found as a father of five that when we trust in God - With a radical trust - And we do our part - God can and does do the impossible…..We just need to learn to trust him…What prevents us from this kind of trust is we do not want to "give up control"…..This mindset limits us because we are all limited…We need to remind ourself God is limitless…..When we give up control and "step out into the deep"…God steps in…..God waits for us in "that space"……As he did with Our Lady….Mary gives us the example…..She was human, just like you and I - She was confused and afraid, just like we are at times……"How can this be, since I have no relations with a man?"…But Mary "stepped past" her fears and put her hand into the hand of God and NEVER looked back….This is what we must do as well…..Step out into the deep!……"May it be done to me according to your word"…..At the statement of Mary the gates of hell trembled!….And when we say that statement to this very day….The gates of hell tremble once again!

PERSONAL NOTES:

21ˢᵗ
Day of Advent

THE CUP MUST BE "EMPTIED AND
THEN FILLED AGAIN"...YOU ARE
THAT CUP - ITS TIME TO "FILL
UP"......THAT IS THE "BIG SECRET"
MY FRIENDS....AND WHEN YOU COME
RIGHT DOWN TO IT.... ITS REALLY NO
SECRET

Today at Holy Mass we hear from the Gospel of St Luke . In the text we hear about Mary's visit to her cousin Elizabeth who needed help Elizabeth was older than Mary and pregnant - So Mary "went in haste" to assist her .This is the entire gospel summarized in a nut-shell .When Catholics are filled with the Holy Spirit - They "go out" and give the Holy Spirit away ."Without cost you have received; without cost you are to give" .When people hear the word "give" they immediately think of money .That is not what I am talking about And that is not what Mary gave away - She gave away "herself" Nothing is more powerful than a self sacrificing witness .This is the clarion call of every Baptized Catholic .To "give yourself away" .What do we get in return? ..True Joy & Deep Peace Pay attention, this is the important part ..When we "die to our self" and "give ourself away", we "make room for God" in our heart And in turn, God fills us with his very self This is the secret my friends "It is in giving that we receive" And I am not talking about money Its far too easy to "write a check" ..I am talking about something far more valuable - The "gift of self" - I am talking about YOU and ME

"He will rejoice over you with gladness, and renew you in his love, He will sing joyfully because of you, as one sings at festivals"

Today's gospel from Mass ended with this statement from Elizabeth to her cousin Mary.................."Blessed are you who believed that what was spoken to you by the Lord would be fulfilled"......Mary took the word of God to heart - She actually believe it...Its so easy to read what Jesus said and take it for granted - Thinking the words do not apply to "me".....Mary did not do that, and nor should we... We need to take Christ at his word....There is great power in the words of Jesus especially when his words are put into action......... Jesus tells us many things in the gospel and far too many people in the world, when they read the words of Christ say to themselves..."This can't be done" - "This is not realistic".....And to a degree they are right...If we try to do what Jesus told us relying upon our own strengthen and natural gifts, we will surely fail...But if we rely upon grace, we can do it....."Whoever believes in me will do the works that I do, and will do greater ones than these, because I am going to the Father"..........When the world witnesses self sacrificial love...The world has no response except to stand in awe...There is no argument against it....Self sacrificial love witnessed penetrates even the hardest of hearts...It speaks to people and communicates what words will never communicate..."I care about you".........."You mean something to me"...........This is how the gospel spreads...The only way it spreads - One person at a time - From me to you......Every Christmas Season Mother Teresa's sisters would have a Christmas party in Lower Manhattan for all the people who lived in the Elliott-Chelsea Housing Projects.....And the sisters would spare no expense...They would cook for days, give gifts, provide a bus for the families and even have us volunteers pick up the elderly....No expense was spared....They welcomed these people as they would welcome Christ himself.....Actions like that speak to the heart....There is an old saying..."People do not care how much you know until they know how much you care"....... The words in the gospel are life giving but just saying the "words" will mean nothing to people unless they "see" the words fleshed out in real time…..This requires self sacrificial love….This is where the "rubber meets the road"…Mary today in the gospel from Mass shows us how to do this…......First - Mary said YES to the angel and as a result she was filled with the Holy Spirit….What happened next?…..She "went out" to help her cousin and in doing so, she "gave away" the Holy Spirit……Here is the take away…We can not give what we do not have…First - We have to be "filled with God"….We do that by daily prayer, fasting and living a Sacramental life…..Only then does the second part happen - The "giving of self" away to others…..This is the "One-Two Punch"…This is the "dynamite" of the Catholic Church…This is what we are all called to do as Catholics…Words don't cut it

"Fear not, O Zion, be not discouraged! The LORD, your God, is in your midst"

Mary today in the Gospel understood..To be a follower of Christ means we must live for others…..Love gives, it never takes….. However, this type of living witness can not be accomplished on our own……Jesus tells us point blank….."Whoever believes in me will do the works that I do, and will do greater ones than these, because I am going to the Father"……Before this happens, the cup must be "emptied and then filled again"…You are that cup - Its time to "fill up"……That is the "big secret" my friends….And when you come right down to it…. Its really no secret

PERSONAL NOTES:

22ᴺᴰ
Day of Advent

OUR STRENGTHEN LIES IN THE
"LITTLE THINGS" - STRIVE TO DO
THEM WELL!

Today at Holy Mass, the last Sunday of Advent, we hear in the second reading from the Letter to the Hebrews something interesting .."Sacrifice and offering you did not desire, but a body you prepared for me; in holocausts and sin offerings you took no delight" .This statement speaks to me because its the "little things" that count the most ..We can so easily lose focus, we all want to go "big things" But God came to us as a little child The birth of the King of Kings took place "below the radar" of the world .More times then not, this is how God works In the "little things" of life .The Holy Family, the first Church, Jesus, Mary and Joseph for thirty years lived their life hidden from the rest of the world The Holy Family did all the things normal families do ..This should tell us something .We need to focus on the "little things" God has placed us exactly where we need to be ..Its in the present moment, in our homes, with our family, with our friends, at work Its there that we live out the gospel message Notice I said "live out" Let the "big things" take care of themselves Concentrate on the "little things" As Scripture tells us .'Well done, good servant! You have been faithful in this very small matter; take charge of ten cities" Our strengthen lies in the "little things" - Strive to do them well!

"Once again, O LORD of hosts, look down from heaven, and see; take care of this vine, and protect what your right hand has planted the son of man whom you yourself made strong"

Next to Jesus and Mary, St Joseph is considered by many to be the holiest of saints...Do you know throughout the entire Bible not one word is record of what St Joseph ever said...St Joseph found his sanctity in performing his day to day duties, serving his wife and children...He did not write books, he did not have a podcast, he did not give lectures in front of big crowds...He was simple and performed the most basic of tasks - But here is the difference - St Joseph did everything in and for God...So much so, he is the Patron Saint of the Universal Church...Just think if we focused on the simple things and lived in the present moment!...Think about how God can mold us if we did just that!.....Jesus tells us in Scripture...."In praying, do not babble like the pagans, who think that they will be heard because of their many words"...I write this because this applies to me!!!.....My wife and I have a very structured prayer life but many times I find that my mind drifts, I say the words but my focus is on something else...Even when I sit before the Blessed Sacrament, my body is there but my mind is somewhere else....I need to learn to live in the present moment - So pray for me!...How much more can God use the time I give him... If I focus.....Our "greatness" is found in small things - Remember that!.....Many people who grew up in Rutherford New Jersey as I did knew Patrick Fahey...Patrick had eight children and I grew up with many of them...He was a simple man and worked as a crossing guard in town after he retired...Everyone knew Patrick... He was so joyful....So full of life.....He always had a "good word" to share with everyone and to be honest with you, everyone was his friend, he talked to everyone!...Patrick raised eight children without a car...He rode his bike to where he worked as a crossing guard after he "retired" and he worked into his eighties...Patrick was a "simple man"...But Patrick was a light that pointed to God...At least for me he did - And I am sure his life's example did the same

for many others….Patrick did all that by living and being simple…
…."Well done, good servant! You have been faithful in this very
small matter; take charge of ten cities"……Our strengthen lies in
the "little things" - I need to remember that!…..The example of
Patrick Fahey's life reminds me and I miss my friend to this day…
That is what saints do…They remind us…They point to Jesus…
They show us the way!

*"May your help be with the man of your right hand, with the
son of man whom you yourself made strong. Then we will no
more withdraw from you; give us new life, and we will call
upon your name."*

The second reading from Mass today tells us…Leave the "big stuff"
to the "fancy people"…Let's stick with doing the "small things"
well….Jesus came to us as a helpless child born in a barn…The
world around Jesus when he was born could care less…They did
not "see" what was happening right in front of their eyes…So it is
when we do not pay attention to the "little things"….We need to
learn - I need to learn to pay attention to the "little things"!!…Like
my old friend Patrick Fahey, who I miss dearly…Patrick paid attention to the "little things" and he did them well…Maybe that is why
he always had a smile on his face - And everyone who encountered
him had a smile too…..Our strengthen lies in the "little things" -
Strive to do them well!

PERSONAL NOTES:

23rd
Day of Advent

"YES, HE IS COMING, SAYS THE LORD OF HOSTS".......THE QUESTION REMAINS....ARE WE PREPARED TO MEET HIM?

Today at Holy Mass, we hear in the first reading from the Prophet Malachi ..This text tells us how God will send Elijah to prepare the people for God .To say that God needs to "prepare" people implies we are all not ready to stand before the Almighty .Our lives are a work in progress "For he is like the refiner's fire, or like the fuller's lye. He will sit refining and purifying silver, and he will purify the sons of Levi, Refining them like gold or like silver" ..Habits are hard to break To break bad habits and acquire virtue takes time and grace This does not happen overnight ..No one is perfect and the first step towards perfection is admitting our faults and weakness - We all have them! ..This is why going to a Sacramental Confession at least once a month is vital ..In doing so, not only are our sins forgiven but we are given grace to overcome "bad habits" (i.e. our sins), which more times then not, we can not break free from on our own - We need God's grace! This is how we grow in virtue ..We need divine assistance - All of us need this assistance! ..The Catholic Church is not a museum for saints, it is hospital for sinners ..Jesus is the divine physician and the Sacraments are the medicine for the world .Malachi the Prophet tells us today .."Yes, he is coming, says the LORD of hosts" .Are we prepared to meet him?

"All the paths of the LORD are kindness and constancy toward those who keep his covenant and his decrees"

What keeps us from peace?…Ask yourself this…Why do we fear change and facing our own faults?…..Fear does not come from God and we must recognize this reality…..Christmas is two days away and the greatest gift we can give to Jesus is our sins in a Sacramental Confession…..The last couple of years I would go to St Patrick's Cathedral in Manhattan to go to Confession before the noon Mass on Fridays (The Cathedral is near my office)…I notice that the same people are always on the line with me…..People struggling to overcome vices and bad habits - As I am - We all have them - And its a process to uproot our "issues" - And the "medicine" we need is God's mercy and grace…This is why Jesus came and walked among us and frankly we ALL need his help to free us from our weakness…Don't believe me - Look around - How is the world doing without God?…..One of the years I went to India I brought over with me a group of third order Franciscans……A Franciscan priest also came with us…Fr Leo was a great baseball played from Texas in his younger years…Believe it or not, he almost made it to the Major Leagues as a second baseman but something must have happened along the way….He felt "the call" and became a priest… Every night after we would work at the various centers around the city of Kolkata serving the poor, the Missionaries of Charity would end the day by exposing the Blessed Sacrament for a Holy Hour in their convent….Both the nuns and the volunteers would attend this event together - It was some sight to behold - An interesting mix of people……….To the suprise of many people reading this reflection, not all the volunteers were practicing Catholics and some of us were, lets just say "rough around the edges" - But I think that is what made the Holy Hour so great!…..I have met Jews, non-believers, hippies, you-name-it in Kolkata, who came to serve the poor with Mother Teresa's sisters…..People come from all over the world to help out of the goodness of their heart…Any way back to my story…On this trip, Fr Leo during each night at the Holy Hour would sit in the far corner hearing confessions…It was always interesting to see who would stand up and go to confession…Sometimes you would see a nun, various volunteers, etc… This one time, this girl with long dreadlocks and covered in tattoos gets up abruptly and walks over and sits with Fr Leo and gave her confession….It was an odd sight to see in many ways because this young girl you would have thought would have been the last person to go to confession by the way see looked (A lesson for all of us not to judge people!)….So there you have it - A Franciscan priest, who was an ex-baseball player from Texas, talking to a hippie girl covered in tattoos in a convent of nuns in India…..Only Jesus can bring people together like that…Speaking personally, it was a beautiful sight to see…..I will always remember it

"Lift up your heads and see; your redemption is near at hand"

Today in the first reading the Prophet Malachi is trying to prepare us for the coming of the Lord…Christmas is coming!….Are we prepared? - And I am not talking about buying one last gift….Have we prepared our hearts for the birth of Christ?…..This is why we should consider going to a Sacramental Confession with a Priest - In fact, make it a habit, go to Confession once a month…..Make this Christmas the greatest Christmas you ever had….Give your self the gift of peace……Its free………….."Refining them like gold or like silver that they may offer due sacrifice to the LORD. Then the sacrifice of Judah and Jerusalem will please the LORD, as in the days of old, as in years gone by"…….Malachi the Prophet tells us today…..."Yes, he is coming, says the LORD of hosts"……. The question remains….Are we prepared to meet him?

PERSONAL NOTES:

24th
Day of Advent

JESUS IS IN OUR MIDST TODAY,
BORN HUMBLE, LOST, ALONE AND
DESPISED....DO WE "SEE" HIM?.....IS
THERE STILL NO ROOM IN THE INN?

Today at Holy Mass in the first reading we hear from the Prophet Samuel who tells us about King David Jesus was born from the line of David ..Similar to Jesus, David was born a "no-body" .."It was I who took you from the pasture and from the care of the flock to be commander of my people Israel" All this happened right under the nose of the world No one gave David a second look as he worked in the fields Similarly, the same thing happened with Jesus . Born in a barn ..Juxtapose the "blindness" of the world to Elizabeth, Mary's cousin ..When Mary greeted her, this is what she said ."When Elizabeth heard Mary's greeting, the infant leaped in her womb, and Elizabeth, filled with the holy Spirit, cried out in a loud voice and said, "Most blessed are you among women, and blessed is the fruit of your womb. And how does this happen to me, that the mother of my Lord should come to me?" Elizabeth immediately knew that God was in her presence So the question we should consider is .How did Elizabeth understand and the rest of the world "missed it" . The birth of Christ took place in real time - Its a historical event .And as his birth was taking place, the Inn Keepers turned Joseph and Mary away They were "blind" How can we ensure we do not "miss it"?

"O Radiant Dawn, splendor of eternal light, sun of justice: come and shine on those who dwell in darkness and in the shadow of death."

Mother Teresa was clear - When her sisters helped the poor around the world, they were directly serving Christ himself in the flesh….These are Mother Teresa's words…."When we touch the sick and needy, we touch the suffering body of Christ"…..She goes on….."Jesus comes to meet us. To welcome him, let us go to meet him: He comes to us in the hungry, the naked, the lonely, the alcoholic, the drug addict, the prostitute, the street beggars. He may come to you or me in a father who is alone, in a mother, in a brother, or in a sister. If we reject them, if we do not go out to meet them, we reject Jesus himself"…….Mother Teresa tells the world very directly, that we are still "blind" and "miss" Jesus in our very midst… He is in the poor she tells us - Or better put, He is the poor walking among us right in front of our eyes, poverty has many disguises, its not always material…..There are many ways to encounter Christ…One of those ways for people of good will to encounter Jesus, without knowing it is Christ is when they serve the poor with their own two hands…There is a great mystery in our service to the poor, which human eyes do not perceive…When we give ourself to others who need our help….."Doors" begin to open in our hearts and our eyes slowly begin to "see"…I have witnessed this many times with people who serve the poor with Mother Teresa sisters around the world…..They may not realize it in real time, but as serve the poor, they are touching the wounds of Christ, when they reach a hand to assist the forgotten, the lost and the marginalized of the world…..In time, those who serve the poor "see"…And this acquired sight leads to the Blessed Sacrament, which is the light of the world

"The daybreak from on high has visited us"

Samuel the prophet reminds us at Mass today, that King David was a no-body and soon Jesus will be born, another "no-body"….

In these two men, great things resulted....And the "sophisticated" world missed it....Mother Teresa also reminds us that we must learn to "see"....And in order to gain our sight, we must extend a hand to others - Giving of our self - Its too easy to give money......
Mother Teresa said it best...."Jesus is the one we take care of, visit, clothe, feed, and comfort every time we do this to the poorest of the poor, to the sick, to the dying, to the lepers, and to the ones who suffer from AIDS.........We should not serve the poor like they were Jesus. We should serve the poor because they are Jesus".....
Jesus is in our midst today, born humble, lost, alone and despised....
Do we "see" him?.....Is there still no room in the Inn?

PERSONAL NOTES:

www.ingramcontent.com/pod-product-compliance
Lightning Source LLC
Chambersburg PA
CBHW070042100426
42740CB00013B/2771